Key Stage Three
Shakespeare
Much Ado About Nothing

This book is for 11-14 year olds.

It's packed with all the really important stuff you need to know about *Much Ado About Nothing* if you want to do well in your Key Stage Three SAT Shakespeare Question.

We've stuck loads of pictures and jokes in to make it more fun — so you'll actually use it.

Simple as that.

What CGP is all about

Our sole aim here at CGP is to produce the highest quality books — carefully written, immaculately presented and dangerously close to being funny.

Then we work our socks off to get them out to you — at the cheapest possible prices.

Contents

SECTION 5 — WRITING AN ESSAY

SECTION 6 — TYPES OF QUESTION

SECTION 7 — THE SET SCENES

Published by Coordination Group Publications Ltd.

Contributors:
Taissa Csáky
Kate Houghton
Tim Major
Kate Redmond
Katherine Reed
Edward Robinson
Elisabeth Sanderson
Alice Shepperson
Gerry Spatharis
Jennifer Underwood
Nicola Woodfin

With thanks to Paula Barnett and Nicola Woodfin for the proofreading.

ISBN: 978 1 84762 019 4

Groovy website: www.cgpbooks.co.uk
Jolly bits of clipart from CorelDRAW®
Printed by Elanders Hindson Ltd, Newcastle upon Tyne.

Preparing Your Answer

Preparation is the key to doing well in your exam. So, before you start writing, plan what you're going to write. This will make everything a lot easier, even if it sounds like loads of extra work.

You Have to Know the Set Scenes Really Well

1) The Shakespeare paper tests how well you know the play.
2) It's all about the set scenes. Your teacher will tell you which the set scenes are — if you ask them nicely...
3) You have to know these scenes like the back of your hand.

Learn your set scenes... or the puppy gets it.

You'll know what bits of the play you have to write about before the exam — which means you won't get any nasty surprises on the day. As long as you've learnt 'em, that is.

Take Time to Plan Your Answers

Planning might seem like a waste of precious exam time. But if you just start writing without planning you'll end up spouting rubbish. Planning makes your answer loads better.

1) Read the question. Check it out carefully. It could be two questions squished into one:

e.g. Q. In Act 2, Scene 3, what is Benedick's opinion of love and how is he made to fall in love with Beatrice?

What is Benedick's opinion of love?   How is he made to fall in love with Beatrice?

2) Read through the scenes again. Look for anything the characters say that will help you answer the question. When you find something useful, underline it. E.g. For the first part of the question above you would look for anything that Benedick says about love.

3) Next, think about what the main points of your essay will be. Make a list.

Do you see my point?

e.g.
• what Benedick thinks about love
• the plan to make Benedick fall in love with Beatrice
• how the others convince Benedick that Beatrice has fallen for him
• how Benedick feels about this "news"
• what he plans to do

4) Include all your main points in the essay. Then you'll be on your way to a good mark.

Preparation, that's what you need...

You'll feel a lot more relaxed once you've got a good plan to fall back on. Once that's sorted you can focus on each point one at a time. This makes the whole exam thing a lot less scary.

Writing Well and Giving Examples

Examiners are a funny lot, but it's easy enough to impress them if you know what makes them tick. Here's a few useful little tricks that'll have them gasping in admiration.

Use Examples To Show You Know Your Stuff

It's crucial that you use examples. They show evidence of the points you're making. As my old granny used to say, "An opinion without an example is like a boy-band without a rubbish dance routine." Or something.

Quotes are really useful examples. Examiners love 'em. Remember to:

I couldn't unlock the key scenes.

1) Start and end quotes with speech marks.
2) Copy out the words exactly as the they are in the play.
3) Explain why the quote is a good example — what does it tell you?

Sort Out Your Writing

1) Sound enthusiastic about the play. Use plenty of adjectives (descriptive words).

The atmosphere in this scene is really tense and electrifying — Shakespeare makes the audience keen to find out what happens to Benedick.

2) Check your spelling and your punctuation.
Otherwise the examiner might not know what you mean.

3) Write in paragraphs. A page that's full of writing with no breaks is tough to read. Remember, a new topic = a new paragraph.

Write About Versions of the Play You've Seen

If you've seen a film or theatre version of the play, you can write about that too — as long as it relates to the question.

This is another good way of sounding interested in the play. Just make sure you mention which version of the play you saw.

Keep in mind that each version can be very different. The costumes, settings and personalities of the characters can all vary.

In the production of the play I saw in Barnsley in 2002, the director, Ivor Megaphone, brought out the humour in this scene by making the actors bump into each other all the time.

I'll make an exam-ple of you...

Exams aren't really that complicated. They ask you a question, you answer it. If you're prepared, there'll be no nasty surprises. Stick to the point, and there's nowt to worry about.

Stage Directions, Acts and Scenes

It's really important you know what <u>stage directions</u>, <u>acts</u> and <u>scenes</u> are. Acts and scenes are like the <u>skeleton</u> of the play, and stage directions tell you what's going on <u>on-stage</u>.

Stage Directions Tell You Who's Doing What

<u>Stage directions</u> tell the actors what to do, e.g. <u>when to come on stage</u> and <u>when to go off</u>. They sometimes say <u>who</u> they have to talk to as well. They're usually written in <u>italics</u> or put in <u>brackets</u>:

The <u>names</u> of the characters are written here to tell you who's <u>speaking</u>.

<u>Swoon</u> — this stage direction means she faints.

LEONATO: Hath no man's dagger here a point for me?

[Hero swoons]

BEATRICE: Why, how now, cousin! Wherefore sink you down?

DON JOHN: Come, let us go. These things, come thus to light,
Smother her spirits up.

[Exeunt Don Pedro, Don John, and Claudio]

Act 4, Scene 1, 109-110

<u>Exeunt</u> means more than one person <u>leaves</u> the stage.

Which way to the station please?

The <u>line numbers</u> often <u>vary</u> in different printed versions of the play — so <u>don't worry</u> if these line numbers don't exactly match your copy.

Remember, plays are supposed to be <u>performed</u>, not read. So <u>stage directions</u> are really helpful for imagining how the play would <u>look on-stage</u>.

Acts and Scenes Split Up the Play

1) The play is divided up into <u>five</u> big chunks called <u>acts</u>. Each act tells us <u>part</u> of the story. Put them all together and you get the <u>whole</u> story.

2) Acts are also divided up into even <u>smaller</u> chunks called <u>scenes</u>. Scenes <u>break up</u> the story. A <u>new</u> <u>scene</u> might be in a <u>different place</u>, at a <u>different</u> <u>time</u>, or with <u>different characters</u>.

E.g. if one scene is set <u>inside</u> Leonato's house, the next scene could be <u>outside</u> the house. Or one scene might be set during the <u>day</u>, and the next at <u>night</u>.

Are you sure this is the right scene?

Stop it, you're making a scene...

<u>Acts</u> and <u>scenes</u> are actually <u>really handy</u>, as they can help you <u>find</u> the speech or bit of action you're looking for. Remember — the play has <u>5 acts</u> and <u>loads of scenes</u>.

Much Ado About Nothing as a Play

Check out these tips and you'll really get to grips with the play.

It's a Play, Not a Novel

It's meant to be acted, not just read. When you read the play, it's hard to imagine what it will look like on stage. Try and see the characters in your mind. Think about:

- what kind of people they are
- how you think they would say their lines
- how they would act

If you want some idea of how the play might look when it's acted out, you could watch it on video or DVD. Your school might have a copy of it — it's worth asking. Just remember: each version will be different.

Sometimes Characters Talk to Themselves

1) In real life, this is odd. In plays, it's normal — it doesn't mean they've gone bananas.

2) The characters talk to themselves to let the audience know what they are thinking and how they are feeling.

3) When someone talks to themself on an empty stage, it's called a soliloquy (or monologue).

4) If someone talks to the audience when there are other people on stage, it'll say [Aside] by their name in the play. The audience can hear what is being said, but the other characters can't.

Much Ado is a Comedy

It has funny bits in it, just like comedies on TV (well, some of them anyway). The characters often play tricks on each other. Most of the comedy comes from:

In Shakespeare's day, comedies were any plays with a happy ending (usually a wedding).

Dogberry

He's a very silly character who tries to use big words when he doesn't really know what they mean.

Benedick and Beatrice

They spend most of the time making fun of each other.

Shakespeare in Yorkshire — Much Ado About Nowt...

If you're not used to reading plays, it's bound to feel odd at first. Remember, it's a comedy so it's bound to be a bit daft — you'll get used to the humour and people talking to themselves.

Odd Language

Some of this <u>old language</u> is hard to get your head round. But once you get the hang of <u>reading it</u> things will become a lot <u>clearer</u>. Just remember these <u>rules</u>:

Don't Stop Reading at the End of a Line

1) Follow the <u>punctuation</u> — read to the <u>end of the sentence</u>, not the end of the <u>line</u>.

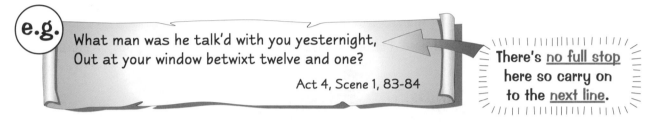

e.g.

What man was he talk'd with you yesternight,
Out at your window betwixt twelve and one?

Act 4, Scene 1, 83-84

There's <u>no full stop</u> here so carry on to the <u>next line</u>.

2) These <u>two lines</u> actually make up <u>one sentence</u>:

What man was he talk'd with you yesternight, out at your window betwixt twelve and one?

3) Most lines start with a <u>capital letter</u> — but this doesn't always mean it's a <u>new sentence</u>.

4) <u>Full stops</u>, <u>question marks</u> and <u>exclamation marks</u> show you where the sentence ends.

Sometimes You Have to Switch the Words Around

1) Shakespeare likes to <u>mess around</u> with the <u>order</u> of words.
It helps him fit the sentences into the <u>poetry</u> (see page 7).

2) If a piece of writing looks like it's <u>back-to-front</u> — <u>don't panic</u>.

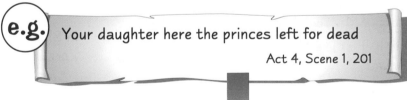

e.g.

Your daughter here the princes left for dead

Act 4, Scene 1, 201

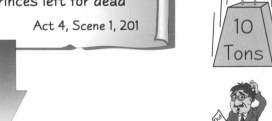

3) <u>Play around</u> with the <u>word order</u> and it'll <u>make sense</u>. What this <u>really</u> says is:

The princes left your daughter here for dead.

Sense make doesn't Shakespeare...

I know Shakespeare's language looks really <u>different</u> to the English we speak, but it's actually <u>pretty similar</u>. Once you've got the <u>word order</u> sorted you're well on the way to <u>sussing it out</u>.

More Odd Language

Shakespeare was around over <u>400 years ago</u> — so the language he uses can seem a bit <u>weird</u>. Some of the words are <u>old words</u> that we <u>don't use any more</u>.

Thou, thee and thy come up a lot

Once you know what these words mean, things get <u>a lot easier</u>. Happy days.

Thou = you

> Didst thou not hear somebody?
> Act 3, Scene 3, 125

Thee = you

> I shall see thee, ere I die...
> Act 1, Scene 1, 229

Thy = your

> What pace is this that thy tongue keeps?
> Act 3, Scene 4, 87

Verbs Can Look Odd

> Hast thou seen the size of this carrot?

Often, all that's different is there's a couple of <u>extra letters</u> on the end of the verb. Take off the <u>t</u> or <u>st</u> and you'll see what they mean.

e.g.

Hath, Hast = has		Wilt = will
Didst = did	Thinkst = think	Speakst = speak

These verbs often go with <u>thou</u>, like this:

> Benedick, didst thou note the daughter of Signor Leonato?
> Act 1, Scene 1, 150

Some Words are Squashed Together

The word <u>it</u> often gets <u>stuck to the next word</u>, and <u>loses the "i"</u>.

e.g.

'twas = it was   'twere = it were
'tis = it is   is't = is it

> 'Tis an outrage!

An i for an i...

<u>Dropping letters</u> from words isn't that strange when you think about it. We still do it in modern English, like when we change <u>it is</u> to <u>it's</u>. Shakespeare just drops <u>different letters</u>.

Poetry

There's lots of <u>poetry</u> in Shakespeare's plays. If you understand the poetry, it'll <u>help you understand</u> some of the reasons behind the <u>strange language</u>.

How to Spot Poetry

<u>Prose</u> means writing that <u>isn't poetry</u> — a <u>lot</u> of Much Ado is written in <u>prose</u>. But there's a lot of <u>poetry</u> too — and <u>here's how to spot it</u>:

> **Poetry has:**
>
> 1) **Capital letters at the start of each line**
>
> 2) **10, 11 or 12 syllables in each line**

A <u>syllable</u> is a unit of sound. The word <u>poetry</u> has 3 syllables – <u>po</u> <u>e</u> <u>try</u>.

Poetry Doesn't Have to Rhyme

1) Some poetry <u>rhymes</u>, some <u>doesn't</u>.

e.g.
> What fire is in mine ears? Can this be true?
> Stand I condemn'd for pride and scorn so much?
> Contempt, farewell and maiden pride, adieu!
> No glory lives behind the back of such.
> > Act 3, Scene 1, 107-110

Each line starts with a <u>capital letter</u>.

This bit of poetry <u>rhymes</u> on <u>alternate lines</u>.

e.g.
> When you went onward on this ended action
> I look'd upon her with a soldier's eye
> That lik'd, but had a rougher task in hand
> Than to drive liking to the name of love:
> > Act 1, Scene 1, 277-280

This <u>doesn't rhyme</u> — but it's <u>still poetry</u>.

2) The language sometimes sounds <u>strange</u> because Shakespeare tries to get <u>each line</u> to contain the <u>right amount of syllables</u>.

3) Poetry is usually used when someone is talking about an <u>emotional topic</u>, like <u>love</u> or <u>hate</u>. But <u>Claudio</u> and <u>Hero</u>, <u>the romantic leads</u> speak in poetry <u>all the time</u>.

4) Poetry is usually only spoken by the <u>upper class</u> families.

You did ask for three silly bulls?

Leann Rimes — with what?

Once you realise you're dealing with <u>poetry</u>, it becomes much easier to work out <u>what it means</u>. And the rules for <u>spotting it</u> are pretty simple — just remember that it doesn't have to rhyme.

Revision Summary

Right, let's see how much you know about Bill Shakespeare and his odd little ways. If you haven't read any of Shakespeare's stuff before, it's easy to be flummoxed by the way he writes. But trust me, the more you read, the easier it gets. If you get stuck on any of these questions, look back through the section to find the answers. Then have another go, without looking back.

1) What's the point of stage directions?
2) What does "swoon" mean?
3) What's the play split up into?

   a) Chapters and verses   b) Nooks and crannies   c) Acts and scenes

4) A play is meant to be:

   a) ignored   b) burnt   c) performed

5) What is a soliloquy?
6) If it says "Aside" by a character's name, who can hear what they're saying?

   a) the other characters   b) the audience   c) Belgians

7) What type of play is Much Ado About Nothing?

   a) comedy   b) tragedy   c) history

8) Which characters are the funniest in Much Ado About Nothing?
9) "A new line of poetry means it's a new sentence." True or false?
10) If a piece of writing doesn't make sense, what should you do?

   a) change the word order   b) phone a friend   c) cry

11) When was Shakespeare around?

   a) 400 years ago   b) 200 years ago   c) 65 million years ago

12) What do these words mean?

   a) thou   b) hath   c) didst   d) 'twas

13) What does each line of poetry start with?
14) How many syllables are there in a line of poetry?
15) Does all poetry rhyme?
16) Which type of characters usually speaks in poetry?
17) Fancy a cuppa?

Am I the only one struggling with the lingo?

Who's Who in the Play

You'll find all the <u>main characters</u> on this page. Some of the names sound <u>foreign</u> — that's because the play's set in <u>Sicily</u> (an island near Italy).

The Happy Couple — Claudio and Hero

It's <u>love at first sight</u> for these two. Then they <u>fall out</u>. Then they <u>get back together</u> again.

CLAUDIO
HERO

Another Happy Couple — Benedick and Beatrice

Benedick and Beatrice are <u>set up</u> by their <u>friends</u> to fall for each other. And it works.

BENEDICK
BEATRICE

Don Pedro — Prince of Aragon

Don Pedro is a <u>Military Commander</u> and the <u>Prince</u>. He's <u>in charge</u> and everyone knows it.

DON PEDRO

They call me the Guv'nor.

LEONATO

Leonato — Governor of Messina

Leonato is <u>Hero's dad</u> and Beatrice's uncle. Most of the <u>action</u> takes place in and around his <u>house</u>.

Don John and his Sidekicks

Don John is the Prince's <u>illegitimate brother</u>. He's the main villain. <u>Borachio</u> helps him with his <u>evil plan</u>. <u>Conrade's</u> just a hanger on.

DON JOHN

BORACHIO

A Bunch of Servants

The two important ones are <u>Margaret</u> and <u>Ursula</u>, Hero's maids. They get involved in the <u>tricks</u> being played.

MARGARET

Dogberry, Verges and The Watch

These are <u>officers of the law</u> in Messina. They're a bit of a <u>comedy act</u>, but thanks to them Don John gets found out.

DOGBERRY

Antonio and Friar Francis

These are more members of Leonato's household. <u>Antonio</u> is <u>Leonato's brother</u>. He and <u>Friar Francis</u> support the family when Hero's <u>wedding</u> goes wrong.

FRIAR FRANCIS

All Don and Dusted...

Ok, there's a lot of <u>characters</u>, and yes, some pretty <u>complicated relationships</u> between them. Don't let that <u>put you off</u> though — you can always <u>look back</u> at this page if you get <u>confused</u>.

Claudio

Claudio is the big <u>love interest</u>. He nearly turns the play into a <u>tragedy</u>, and his <u>wedding</u> is part of the <u>happy ending</u>. You need to know about his character for your <u>exam</u>.

Claudio's Very *Proud* — and *Romantic*

1) Claudio is a <u>Count</u> from Florence. That means he's an <u>aristocrat</u>. He's also a <u>good mate</u> of <u>Don Pedro</u> — he mixes in <u>powerful circles</u>.

2) He's <u>popular</u> and <u>respected</u> — even Beatrice calls him "<u>noble Claudio</u>". A messenger tells us how <u>brave</u> he's been in <u>battle</u>. He's quite a catch.

3) When he plans to <u>marry Hero</u>, everyone's pleased. She's from a <u>decent family</u> and Claudio's really <u>keen</u> on her.

> CLAUDIO: In mine eye she is the sweetest lady that ever I looked on.
> Act 1 Scene 1, 165-166

4) When Don John and his cronies persuade him that Hero <u>isn't a virgin</u>, he's furious. He feels publicly <u>humiliated</u>. He's just as upset about his <u>loss of face</u> as he is about the thought of Hero being <u>unfaithful</u>. That's partly why he <u>rejects</u> her so publicly at the wedding.

He's Easily *Fooled*

Look, a triceratops.

Where?

Claudio's certainly a bit <u>gullible</u> at times. He lets <u>Don Pedro</u> talk to Hero for him. Then, when <u>Don John</u> lies that <u>Don Pedro</u> is <u>after Hero</u> for himself, he <u>believes him</u> immediately. Claudio goes moping off saying you <u>can't trust your friends</u> in love.

When <u>Don John</u> says Hero's been <u>unfaithful</u>, Claudio immediately believes him — even though Don John has already been caught out <u>telling porkies</u>.

He *Learns* His *Lesson*

1) He's treated Hero so badly, he has to <u>earn his right</u> to marry her. You can tell he feels <u>guilty</u>. After <u>Borachio's confession</u>, Claudio says, "I have drunk poison whiles he uttered it." (Act 5, Scene 1, 233)

2) He <u>takes his punishment</u> too. For someone who has a lot of pride, he has to do a lot of public <u>grovelling</u>. Leonato makes him tell everyone that he was <u>wrong</u> and Hero is <u>innocent</u>.

> CLAUDIO: ...Choose your revenge yourself;
> Impose me to what penance your invention
> Can lay upon my sin.
> Act 5, Scene 1, 259-261

Well there's a turn-up.

You chose number 3, Hero from Messina.

Leonato's BLIND DATE

3) He humbly agrees to marry Leonato's <u>mystery woman</u>, who could be anybody. Lucky for him it turns out to be <u>Hero</u>. He's a lot more <u>mature</u> by the end of the play.

You can Count on Claudio...

He's a man of <u>contrasts</u>, our Claudio. <u>Brave</u>, <u>proud</u> — but <u>foolish</u>, and really <u>cruel</u> to Hero. He <u>gets it right</u> in the end though, 'cos overall he's a <u>decent bloke</u>. Nobody's perfect, after all.

Hero

Hero is the <u>object of Claudio's affection</u>. Unlike Claudio, she <u>doesn't change</u> much during the course of the play — she's pretty much <u>perfect</u> to start with. Don't you just love her?

She Doesn't Have Much Control Over Her Life

This'll show him.

1) Hero's a <u>well-behaved</u> daughter — she does as she's told. When her dad, Leonato, thinks Don Pedro is going to <u>propose</u>, he tells Hero she <u>has to accept</u>. She <u>doesn't protest</u>. She just stands there, silently.

2) During the play, <u>Don Pedro</u> courts her — so he can give her to <u>Claudio</u>. Then Claudio <u>rejects her</u> and hands her back to Leonato. Later, Leonato offers her to <u>Claudio</u> to marry — properly this time. Pass the parcel anyone?

3) She's bit <u>weedy</u> at times. You expect her to <u>fight back</u> when Claudio <u>dumps her</u> at their wedding. But she <u>faints</u> instead. D'oh.

She's Innocent and Sensitive

1) <u>Hero</u> was a <u>classic name</u> for a <u>romantic heroine</u> in Shakespeare's time. Her character is fairly typical as well — <u>passive</u>, <u>docile</u> and <u>innocent</u>.

2) She's very <u>inexperienced</u> in love. When Margaret makes <u>suggestive comments</u> on the morning of the wedding, Hero's <u>shocked</u>. It makes the <u>lies</u> about her seem all the more <u>ridiculous</u>.

> HERO:　　　　　　... my heart is exceeding heavy.
> MARGARET: 'Twill be heavier soon by the weight of a man.
> HERO:　Fie upon thee! art not ashamed?
> > Act 3, Scene 4, 22-24

3) She's <u>gutted</u> when Claudio claims that she's slept with another man. It's <u>humiliating</u> and <u>degrading</u> for someone who's really as <u>pure</u> as she is. And being called a "<u>rotten orange</u>" by your <u>fiancé</u> is a bit harsh, I reckon.

She's Quite Different to Beatrice

Make us a cuppa, luv.

Ok, honey.

1) Hero is <u>respectful</u>, <u>gentle</u>, <u>modest</u>, and <u>obedient</u> — you <u>can't</u> say that about her cousin <u>Beatrice</u>. Hero's still pretty <u>starry-eyed</u> about love and a teeny bit <u>critical</u> of Beatrice's attitude.

2) Hero and Claudio are a <u>traditional</u> couple for Shakespeare's times, as <u>the man is in charge</u> — they're <u>not equals</u> like Beatrice and Benedick. You could say they are fairly <u>bland</u>.

3) Hero <u>hardly says a word</u> until Act 2. She's especially <u>silent</u> around <u>men</u> — unlike Beatrice, who's never lost for words. We do see a bit of <u>spark</u> from her when she <u>tricks Beatrice</u> into falling in love though.

We Don't Need Another Hero...(no really, we don't)

Poor old Hero. She has a really <u>hard time</u> of it — but then again, she <u>never</u> really <u>stands up for herself</u>. The <u>differences</u> between her and <u>Beatrice</u> are pretty crucial to the play.

Benedick and Beatrice

These two are definitely <u>main characters</u> too. It's almost certain your exam will ask you about <u>at least one</u> of them. They're a <u>surprising</u> couple, and they have a <u>fiery relationship</u>.

Benedick *is a bit of a* Comedian

1) Benedick is a mate of <u>Don Pedro</u> and <u>Claudio</u>. He's a <u>soldier</u>, just back from war, where he was <u>honourable</u> and <u>brave</u>.

2) He's <u>cynical</u> about <u>women</u> and <u>love</u> — and says he'll <u>never marry</u>. He's a <u>man of action</u> — not a soppy, romantic lover. He's pretty <u>sure of himself</u> to start with.

3) Benedick's a <u>performer</u>. He loves to entertain the others with his <u>tall stories</u> and <u>insults</u>. He <u>winds up</u> Claudio and Beatrice. He's dead <u>competitive</u> too. He and Beatrice are always trying to <u>outdo</u> each other. They're a <u>perfect match</u>.

> BEATRICE: I wonder that you will still be talking, Signior Benedick. Nobody marks you.
> BENEDICK: What, my dear Lady Disdain! are you yet living?
> *Act 1, Scene 1, 103-105*

A funny thing happened to me on the way to the battlefield...

4) For someone with <u>plenty to say</u>, he has a lot of <u>trouble</u> when he tries to <u>write his feelings down</u>. His <u>love poem</u> to Beatrice is <u>rubbish</u>, and he knows it. He has to get <u>Margaret</u> to <u>help</u> him.

5) There's a <u>serious side</u> to him too. He's quite <u>vulnerable</u> once he starts to fall in love. The others find him <u>easy to trick</u>. He <u>wants to believe</u> Beatrice loves him. He also has his <u>loyalty tested</u> when Beatrice asks him to kill Claudio.

Beatrice *is* Tough *– but even she* Falls in Love

1) Beatrice is an <u>orphan</u>. She's been brought up by her uncle, <u>Leonato</u>. She's <u>witty</u> and <u>confident</u>, which is <u>unusual for a woman</u> at that time — just compare her to <u>Hero</u>. She's as <u>determined</u> as Benedick that she'll <u>never get married</u>.

> BEATRICE: I had rather hear my dog bark at a crow than a man swear he loves me.
> *Act 1, Scene 1, 116-118*

2) Despite her confidence, Beatrice <u>does care</u> about what <u>other people think</u> of her. She's a bit <u>upset</u> when she overhears <u>Hero</u> and <u>Ursula</u> say she's <u>proud</u> and <u>scornful</u>.

3) We also get to see how <u>loyal</u> Beatrice can be. She's <u>really angry</u> when <u>Claudio lets Hero down</u> — and determined to get <u>revenge</u>. She asks Benedick to <u>prove his love</u> by <u>killing Claudio</u>.

"Proud and scornful" am I? PAH!

4) Beatrice <u>won't be controlled</u> by any man — she wants someone who's her <u>equal</u>. Enter <u>Benedick</u>. They're very <u>similar</u> — they're both lively, talkative and competitive. They hide their feelings behind <u>insults</u> — but behind it all, they really <u>fancy each other</u>.

Benny and Beatie — *characters out of* Corrie?

Unlike Claudio and Hero, <u>Benedick</u> and <u>Beatrice</u> are <u>far</u> from the ideal <u>happy couple</u>. They <u>bicker</u>, <u>insult</u> each other — then get <u>married</u>. Surely they've got that the wrong way round...?

Don Pedro and Leonato

We've had a look at the lovers — now for the big guns. These two both have a lot of power over what happens to the other characters. You need to know a bit about both of them for the exam.

Don Pedro is Royalty — He's Firm but Fair

1) Don Pedro is the Prince of Aragon. He's the highest ranking person in the play. He arrives in Messina straight from winning a battle and everyone admires and respects him. He's Leonato's guest — but it's Don Pedro who's in charge.

2) Like Claudio, Don Pedro's a proud man. When sneaky Don John lies about Hero, he knows Don Pedro won't want to be linked to a shameful marriage. Don Pedro's as worried about his own reputation as he is for Claudio's.

I'M THE KING OF THE WORLD!

Don't you mean "Prince of Aragon"?

Same thing.

> D. PEDRO: I stand dishonour'd, that have gone about
> To link my dear friend to a common stale.
> Act 4, Scene 1, 64-65

common stale = prostitute

3) Don Pedro's got power, and he likes to stick his oar in. But unlike his no-good brother Don John, Don Pedro wants people to be happy. He insists on being in on getting Claudio and Hero together. He's also in charge of the plan to make Beatrice and Benedick fall in love.

Leonato's a Father Figure

You're like a father to me.

Oh yeah...

That's because I am your father.

1) Leonato is Hero's dad. He's also Governor of Messina so he's quite rich and important. But he still feels honoured to have Don Pedro staying in his house.

2) Everyone respects Leonato — and he wants it to stay that way. When Claudio rejects Hero, Leonato's first reaction is anger about his own loss of reputation. He feels so ashamed that he says he wishes Hero would die.

3) Like Don Pedro, Leonato's a well-meaning ruler — but he expects obedience from his household. He uses his power for good. He gives Claudio some strict rules to follow to put things right with Hero — but he's not out to punish him.

4) Leonato is generous and affectionate. He's clearly proud of Hero, which is why the accusations bother him so much. He's fond of his niece Beatrice too — even though she's always teasing him. He's quite an emotional chap. He even challenges young Claudio to a duel. All in all, he deserves his happy ending.

Putting the Mess in Messina...

Don Pedro's certainly a bit of a control freak, and maybe a touch self-obsessed — but overall he's a good egg. Leonato's a decent enough fella too — if a touch rash at times, bless 'im...

Don John

Don John <u>doesn't say much</u>, but he makes things <u>happen</u>. He tricks Claudio and makes him reject Hero. He's a <u>contrast</u> to most of the other characters — and quite <u>complex</u>.

He's Born to Cause Trouble

1) In stage directions, Shakespeare calls him '<u>John the Bastard</u>'. He's not just being rude. It means he was <u>born outside marriage</u> — and this is important. <u>Illegitimate children</u> in Shakespeare plays are usually <u>baddies</u> — Don John is <u>no exception</u>.

2) Don Pedro, his brother, is the one who will <u>inherit</u> the <u>family fortune</u> — Don John will get <u>nothing</u>. He's an <u>outsider</u>. The audience expect him to <u>break the rules</u> — and he doesn't disappoint them.

Who? Oooh.. YES that's right. I am Don Juan.

3) He's <u>jealous</u>, <u>bad-tempered</u> and <u>bitter</u>. He's always <u>scheming</u> — he tells <u>Claudio</u> that <u>Don Pedro</u> is trying to <u>get Hero for himself</u>, but that doesn't work. So he tells lies about Hero <u>instead</u>. You've got to admit he's <u>determined</u>.

4) Even the other characters spot how <u>miserable</u> and <u>sour</u> he is. His own mate, <u>Borachio</u>, calls him "<u>the devil my master</u>". Let's face it, you'd probably feel like being <u>bad</u> if that's what everyone seemed to <u>expect</u>.

At least he's Honest...well, sort of

<u>ON THE ONE HAND</u> — Lots of other characters keep <u>changing their minds</u>, but Don John is the <u>same</u> all the way through — <u>ruthless and destructive</u>. And he <u>admits</u> it.
He tells Conrade "I cannot hide what I am" (Act 1 Scene 3, 11). You almost admire him for it. Almost...

> DON JOHN: it must not be denied but I am a plain-dealing villain.
> Act 1, Scene 3, 27-28

<u>BUT THEN AGAIN</u> — He's <u>cunning</u> and <u>tells lies</u> brilliantly. He knows Don Pedro and Claudio probably <u>won't believe him</u> about Hero — and he <u>says so</u>. This makes him seem more <u>sincere</u>. He follows it up with some <u>convincing details</u> — all untrue. He's bad, but he's definitely <u>not stupid</u>.

He Comes to a Sticky End

Once his second dastardly plan goes wrong, Don John <u>runs away</u>. At Claudio's and Hero's <u>wedding</u> — the <u>proper</u> one — we hear that he's been <u>caught</u>. But Benedick tells Don Pedro to leave him until tomorrow. His <u>capture</u> is just another part of everyone else's <u>happy ending</u>.

And I woulda' gotten away with it too, if it hadn't been for you meddlin' Watchmen.

I'm not bitter — actually, I am...

Don John fits the mould of the <u>baddie</u> in a Shakespeare comedy — <u>cunning</u>, <u>clever</u>, and nasty for the <u>sake of being nasty</u>. Without the <u>trouble</u> he causes, I reckon the play would be pretty <u>dull</u>.

Other Characters

You know about the main characters now. Here's a few of the others. Some of them are pretty important to the plot, so it's best know where they fit in.

Leonato's Household

The resemblance is uncanny...

1) Margaret is one of Hero's maids. Margaret is Borachio's girlfriend — he makes her dress up as Hero to trick Claudio into thinking Hero's been unfaithful.

2) Ursula is another maid. She helps Hero trick Beatrice into thinking Benedick is in love with her.

3) Antonio is Leonato's brother. We don't know much about him, except that he's quite old. He's furious when Claudio dumps Hero — he even challenges Claudio to a fight. Claudio doesn't take him seriously though.

4) Friar Francis is supposed to marry Claudio and Hero — he's there when it all goes wrong. He's the one who persuades Leonato that Hero is innocent. He also comes up with the plan to tell everyone Hero's dead, while they sort things out — pretty sneaky for a holy man.

Don John has Two Cronies

Borachio is Don John's sidekick. He gets paid to help with the plot against Hero. He's arrested when the Watch catch him boasting about what he's done. At first he denies everything — but later he breaks down and admits it to Don Pedro.

Conrade is another of Don John's followers. He's the one Borachio is boasting to, and he gets arrested as well.

The Watch are a Bunch of Bumbling Policemen

1) Dogberry is in charge of this lot. He's helped by his deputy, Verges. Dogberry's the chief constable and he's quite full of himself. He means well but he makes a fool of himself by trying to sound too clever.

You're under arrest.

Am I 'eck.

2) Dogberry's Watchmen, led by George Seacoal, arrest Borachio and find out about Don John's plot. At this point they could stop the whole plot — but Dogberry and Verges mess up the explanation so Leonato doesn't take it seriously. Oops.

3) It's the Sexton — acting as a kind of town clerk — who finally gets to the truth. The Sexton helps Dogberry and Verges with the questioning. He sends for the rest of the Watch, who tell him what they heard and the Sexton reports to Leonato.

Watch this — we're rubbish...

All you really need to know about the Watchmen is they're the ones who arrest Borachio and Conrade. Dogberry's silliness balances out the darker side of the play — it is a comedy after all.

Revision Summary

You need to be confident about who all the characters are and why they're important. There are some pretty complicated relationships in there — once you've sussed out who does what to who, you can get on with writing cracking essays. If you're not clear about this stuff, studying the play will be harder than dragging Dawn French up Mount Snowdon wearing flip-flops. Check you can answer all these questions.

1) Who's Claudio's pal?

   a) Don John   b) Don Pedro   c) Don King

2) Who tells Claudio that Hero's been unfaithful?

3) Why does Don Pedro court Hero?

   a) So he can give her to Claudio.   b) Because he wants her for himself.   c) For a laugh.

4) In what way are Claudio and Hero a typical couple of Shakespeare's time?

5) Where have Benedick, Claudio and Don Pedro just returned from?

   a) Fighting in a war   b) France   c) Tesco

6) Who's Beatrice's uncle?

7) How does Beatrice plan to get revenge on Claudio?

   a) She kills him.

   b) She asks Benedick to kill him.

   c) She puts itching powder in his pants.

8) What's Don Pedro's title?

9) What do the other characters think of Don Pedro?

10) Who's Leonato's daughter?

11) How's Don John described in the stage directions?

   a) John the Lovely   b) John the Slightly Irritating   c) John the Bastard

12) When Don John tells lies about Hero, how does he make himself seem more sincere to Don Pedro and Claudio?

13) What are Hero's two maids called?

14) Who are Don John's cronies?

15) Who are the Watch?

   a) Policemen

   b) Doctors

   c) Website designers

Got your ponies for you.

I'm smiling but I'm not happy.

Love and Marriage

Love's a big part of the story in *Much Ado* — if Beatrice and Benedick and Hero and Claudio didn't fall in love it wouldn't be much of a story at all. Here's what you need to know about LURVE...

Getting Married *was Really* Important

Nowadays, lots of films end with the main characters falling in love. In Shakespeare's day people were more religious and traditional. The main characters had to fall in love and get married too. That's how *Much Ado* ends — with the main characters falling in love and getting married.

Help us. We're sinking...

In *Much Ado* most of the characters think love is a good thing and do their best to get Hero and Beatrice married off. But there are other views of marriage in the play too — a lot of the jokes Benedick makes early on are about partners being unfaithful and making each other look foolish.

The Play Has *Different Ideas About* "True Love"

Claudio and Hero end up falling in love and getting married. Beatrice and Benedick end up falling in love and getting married. But the way the two couples do it is very different:

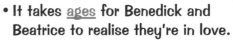

CLAUDIO & HERO
- For Claudio it's love at first sight.
- Claudio's too shy to talk to Hero himself and has to rely on Don Pedro's help.
- Hero doesn't say much either, she just goes along with it.

> *Claudio's love for Hero is conventional and romantic. He wants to believe Hero's completely perfect — but he doesn't really get to know Hero, so it's easy for Don John to trick him into believing the worst of her.*

BEATRICE & BENEDICK
- It takes ages for Benedick and Beatrice to realise they're in love.
- They don't like soppiness so without the trick they'd probably never get together.
- All the flirting's done through clever talk.
- Beatrice and Benedick play equal parts in their relationship — there's no boss.

> *Benedick and Beatrice's relationship is much more realistic than Claudio and Hero's. After all the arguing and teasing, Benedick and Beatrice really know each other. When they fall in love it's easy for them to trust each other and get along.*

Love Can be More *Down-to-Earth* Too

The Benedick-Beatrice and Claudio-Hero couples have one big thing in common — they treat being in love as a very serious, important emotion.

The only other couple in the play, Borachio and Margaret, give you another contrast. They don't talk about getting married, and Margaret makes some pretty crude jokes about sex. For these two, being in love is all about having a good time and there's no need to take it too seriously.

...go together like a horse and carriage...

Most people want to end up married, so most people like watching plays and films about how people fall in love and get married. If you ever decide to write a script, don't forget the love interest.

Honour and Reputation

Much Ado About Nothing was written in about 1600. The way people behaved was very different back then. You need to know a bit about this stuff for the play to make proper sense.

Everyone Had a Place in Society

Class divisions were strict in Shakespeare's day — posh noblemen with titles didn't go round marrying milkmaids, and servants and other workers had to be respectful towards richer, posher people.

1) In the play, Leonato, Antonio, Hero, Beatrice, Benedick, Claudio and Don Pedro are from the posh ruling class. They talk nicely and most of the time they're quite dignified.

2) Dogberry and his chums are from much lower down in society — Shakespeare and his audience thought it was OK to laugh at the way they talk and behave.

3) Don John's place in society is more tricky. His mother and father weren't married — he's illegitimate. He's got a title ('Don' means something like 'Sir') but he doesn't get as much respect as his half-brother Don Pedro.

What Other People Thought Really Mattered

My girlfriend's fat is she?

To keep your place in society, you had to look after your reputation. If you behaved badly and got a bad reputation you wouldn't get as much respect from other people.

e.g. Part of the reason Leonato's upset when Claudio accuses Hero of not being a virgin is it's bad for Leonato's reputation.

Leonato challenges Claudio to a scrap because he feels Claudio's accusations are a personal insult — if he fights Claudio and wins it will prove the insult is false.

Beatrice and Benedick are too proud to fall in love at first. They go on about marriage being for losers, and they don't want to look silly by changing their minds.

Women Had to Know Their Place

Another massive difference between Shakespeare's day and now is the way girls and women were expected to behave. Women and girls were expected to be sweet and obedient.

1) A girl was expected to be a virgin when she got married. That's why it's such a big deal when it seems Hero's been having an affair.

2) In *Much Ado* it's the men who do serious work as soldiers and politicians — Hero and Beatrice aren't expected to work at all.

3) When Claudio accuses Hero of being unfaithful everyone listens to him. His word counts for more than Hero's or Beatrice's because he's a man. Leonato only starts to believe Hero could be innocent when Benedick suggests it.

4) Compared to Hero, Beatrice stands out as feisty and independent. But even she can't kill Claudio herself — she has to ask Benedick to do it.

My reputation's in tatters — lend me a needle...

Well, I can safely say I wouldn't want to be a young woman in 1600. No thank you. Unless I was someone like Beatrice — she says what she wants, does what she wants and gets away with it.

Tricks and Disguises

If you've ever tried balancing a bucket of water on a door or putting a plastic sugar cube in your grandad's tea, you'll know the <u>joy of tricks</u> — and that they don't always work <u>in the real world</u>...

Comedies in Shakespeare's Day were Full of Tricks

These are the main <u>tricks</u> in *Much Ado*...

Beatrice pretends she doesn't know she's dancing with Benedick. *Act 2, Scene 1*

Claudio and Don Pedro make Benedick believe that Beatrice is in love with him. *Act 2, Scene 3*

Ursula and Hero make Beatrice believe Benedick is in love with her. *Act 3, Scene 1*

Don John's trick on Don Pedro and Claudio — making them believe Hero's unfaithful. *Act 3, Scene 3*

Leonato pretends that Hero is her 'cousin' at the second wedding. *Act 5, Scene 4*

The weird thing about the tricks is that <u>everyone</u> falls for them. The characters are quick to <u>believe in appearances</u> — they don't bother to scratch the surface and find out what's <u>really going on</u>.

Sometimes the end result of a trick is quite <u>good</u>, like <u>bringing Benedick and Beatrice together</u>.

Other tricks have really <u>terrible results</u> — Hero <u>nearly dies of shock</u> when Claudio accuses her of being unfaithful.

Some of the tricks really don't look very convincing...

In <u>Act 2, Scene 1</u> Beatrice dances with Benedick. Benedick's wearing a mask. Beatrice <u>pretends</u> not to know who she's dancing with and says all sorts of rude things about Benedick.

<u>We</u> know that Beatrice knows she's dancing with Benedick, but he can't work it out. <u>Playing tricks</u> was a <u>standard storyline</u> in Shakespeare's day — you just have to <u>take it for granted</u> that the characters fall for the tricks.

Characters in the Play are Fooled by Appearances too

In *Much Ado* not everything is as it seems...

At the beginning of the play Benedick and Beatrice <u>seem</u> like people who will never fall in love or marry... but that's exactly what happens.

At first Claudio <u>seems</u> to deeply love Hero... but then he gives up on her in a twinkling of an eye when Don John tricks him.

Hero <u>seems</u> to have betrayed Claudio... but he was completely wrong.

The message of the play could be that <u>YOU CAN'T TRUST IN APPEARANCES</u>.

That all seems fairly straightforward — or does it...

This play's <u>tricktastic</u>. Tricks <u>everywhere</u> and nothing's quite what it seems. Shakespeare puts lots of stuff about <u>not trusting in appearances</u> into the language too — it's a big theme in *Much Ado*.

<table>
<tr><td>ACT 1
SCENES 1, 2 & 3</td><td># What Happens in Act One</td></tr>
</table>

Are you sitting comfortably? Then <u>get on with it</u> and use the rest of this section to <u>learn the story</u>.

Scene One — Claudio's in Love with Hero

In this scene all the main characters gather at <u>Leonato's swanky house</u> in Messina.

1 Don Pedro's on his way to Messina
Don Pedro's been fighting a war against his half-brother Don John. A messenger tells Leonato that Don Pedro won the war and he's coming to visit with a brave young chap called Claudio. Lines 1-27

2 Beatrice asks after Benedick
Beatrice asks the messenger how Benedick did in the war, in a jokey way. Leonato says that Beatrice and Benedick always take the mick out of each other. Lines 28-87

3 Don Pedro and his men arrive
While Leonato and Don Pedro talk in private, Beatrice and Benedick chat – they both say they can't be bothered with love. Everyone's invited to stay at Leonato's house. Lines 88-149

4 Claudio tells Benedick his secret
Claudio and Benedick are left alone together. Claudio says he's in love with Hero. When Don Pedro comes back, Benedick tells him about Claudio's confession. Claudio's too shy to talk to Hero, so Don Pedro says he'll do the talking at the ball tonight. Lines 150-308

Scene Two — Antonio says Don Pedro loves Hero

1 Antonio tells Leonato about a rumour he's heard
Antonio tells Leonato that Don Pedro wants to marry Hero. Leonato's dead chuffed. He asks Antonio to go and give Hero some advance warning. Lines 1-21

2 The musicians arrive
Antonio's son and some musicians arrive, ready to play at the party. Lines 22-25

Antonio's got the wrong end of the stick — it's <u>Claudio</u> who loves Hero.

Scene Three — Don John Feels Like Making Trouble

Wedding bells, schmedding bells. The fun stops here.

1 Don John is in a bad mood
Conrade asks Don John why he's so gloomy — and says that if he's not careful then Don Pedro will think he wasn't serious about patching up their quarrel at the end of the war. Lines 1-39

2 Don John decides to spoil the wedding
Borachio comes in from the party. He tells Don John that Don Pedro's going to chat Hero up for Claudio. Don John decides to do what he can to spoil the wedding plans. Lines 40-70

Don Pedro — the Shakespearean version of Dateline...

So there you have it — all the fun and excitement of Act One. Use these pages to really <u>get to know the story</u> and your key scenes should start to make a whole lot more sense.

What Happens in Act Two

It's the beginning of <u>Act Two</u>. Your Maltesers are nearly finished and you're wishing you'd brought a tissue. And I bet you're sitting on the <u>edge of your seat</u> wondering whether Claudio and Hero are going to hit it off. Or maybe not. They're a bit dull really. I wouldn't invite them around to my house.

Scene One — the Party

Everyone except moody old Don John has had dinner, and it's time for a <u>dance</u>.
All the men are wearing <u>masks</u>, which creates a spot of <u>confusion</u>.

Don Pedro's going to propose tonight. Say yes, sweetie.

Yes, sweetie.

1 Post-dinner chit-chat
Leonato, Antonio, Beatrice and Hero are chatting after supper. Beatrice says Don John's so sour, he gives her indigestion. Leonato tells her she'll never marry if she carries on being so feisty. Beatrice says it doesn't matter. Leonato reminds Hero that Don Pedro's going to propose tonight. Beatrice tells Hero not to say yes unless she likes him. When the rest of the guests come in, Leonato and Antonio put on their masks. Lines 1-78

2 Everyone pairs off for dancing
Don Pedro asks Hero to dance. He flirts with her and they dance away. Beatrice dances with Benedick, but pretends not to know who he is behind the mask. She tells him Benedick's jokes aren't very funny. Lines 79-144

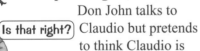

Benedick is so NOT funny.

Is that right?

3 Don John starts spreading evil vibes
Don John talks to Claudio but pretends to think Claudio is Benedick. He tells Claudio Don Pedro's in love with Hero. Don John and Borachio go to get something to eat, leaving Claudio to fret about what he's been told. Lines 145-159

4 Claudio tells Benedick his troubles
Claudio's convinced that Don Pedro's cheated him and is trying to get Hero for himself. Benedick comes to tell Claudio that Hero's agreed to marry Claudio, but Claudio won't believe him and storms off. Lines 160-187

Benedick <u>stomps off</u> because he's too annoyed to speak to Beatrice.

5 Benedick explains to Don Pedro
Benedick tells Don Pedro that Claudio thinks Don Pedro has been chatting up Hero for himself. He also tells Don Pedro how upset he is about Beatrice's insults. Claudio and Beatrice come in and Benedick makes a speedy exit. Lines 188-258

6 Don Pedro sorts things out with Claudio
Don Pedro tells off Beatrice for being so harsh with Benedick, but she's not sorry for what she's done. Then he tells Claudio he really *was* trying to help him marry Hero and she's happy to go ahead with the wedding. Claudio's over the moon. Hero doesn't say anything — she's too shy. Beatrice says she'd marry a man like Don Pedro, but he's too good for her so she won't marry at all. Lines 259-319

7 Don Pedro and Leonato matchmake
When Beatrice has gone, Don Pedro has an idea — he thinks Beatrice and Benedick would make a good couple. There's a week to go until Claudio and Hero's wedding, and Don Pedro sets himself a challenge to get Beatrice and Benedick to fall in love by the end of the week. Lines 320-365

**ACT 2
SCENES 2 & 3**

What Happens in Act Two

Onwards and upwards — here's what happens in <u>the rest of Act Two</u>...

Scene Two — Don John & Borachio Hatch a Plan

1 Don John gets some help from Borachio
Don John is really annoyed about Claudio's wedding. He's determined to stop it. Borachio says he's got a plan. Lines 1-32

2 Borachio's plan
Borachio will stand outside Hero's bedroom window the night before the wedding, and pretend to call Hero out. Really it will be Margaret, his girlfriend, dressed up as Hero. Don John will have Don Pedro and Claudio hiding nearby. When they see 'Hero' talking to Borachio they won't believe she's an innocent virgin anymore and the wedding will be off. Lines 33-56

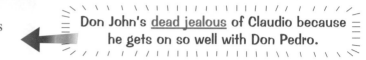
Don John's <u>dead jealous</u> of Claudio because he gets on so well with Don Pedro.

Nice one.

Me... Margaret... Hero's clothes... hide in orchard... wedding off... You happy...

Scene Three — Benedick Falls for a Trick

This is the first of those slightly <u>unconvincing tricks</u>. Benedick hides in a hedge to <u>eavesdrop</u>, and thinks he's got away with it, but the others <u>know he's there</u> all along.

1 Benedick listens in on a conversation
Benedick's alone in the orchard thinking about how much Claudio's changed now he's in love. He hears Don Pedro, Leonato, Claudio and Balthasar coming and decides to listen in on their conversation from a hiding place in a bush. Lines 1-36

2 Don Pedro, Leonato and Claudio set a trap
Don Pedro, Leonato and Claudio all saw Benedick hiding and decide to play a trick. Balthasar sings a love song. Meanwhile, Benedick smirks at how much Claudio's enjoying the music. After the song, Balthasar goes. Lines 37-89

<u>Balthasar</u> is Don Pedro's musician.

3 Benedick takes the bait
Don Pedro asks Leonato whether it's true Beatrice is in love with Benedick. Benedick's gobsmacked. Leonato says Beatrice doesn't dare say anything because she's sure Benedick would turn her down. When the tricksters think Benedick's heard enough they move away. Lines 90-211

4 Benedick's over the moon
Benedick is sure he's not being tricked. He's really happy that Beatrice is in love with him and starts thinking about marrying her. Lines 212-237

5 Beatrice calls Benedick for dinner
Beatrice is her usual self when she tells Benedick that dinner's ready, but Benedick is sure he can see signs that she's in love with him. Lines 238-254

Nope, it's absolutely, definitely, certainly not a trick.

Act Two — bless you...

Benedick's meant to be so witty and clever, but in Scene Three he just acts like a big <u>sucker</u>. How could he not realise he was being set up... it wouldn't happen in real life, but then this <u>is</u> a <u>play</u>...

What Happens in Act Three

Claudio's in love with Hero and Hero's in love with Claudio so that's all sorted (for the moment). Benedick's in love with Beatrice. So Beatrice is next in line at the *Much Ado* Love Parade.

Scene One — Beatrice is Fooled by Hero and Ursula

I feel awful. I had no idea.

Everyone's been talking about it.

They don't **really** think she's hard-hearted — it's all part of the wind up.

1 Hero and Ursula plan a trick for Beatrice
Hero sends her servant Margaret to find Beatrice. She tells Margaret to say Hero and Ursula are in the orchard, gossiping about Beatrice, and she should go and listen in. Lines 1-22

2 Beatrice falls for the trick
Beatrice hides in the orchard. She hears Hero and Ursula saying how much Benedick loves Beatrice and what a shame it is that she's so hard-hearted — she'll never return Benedick's love. Lines 23-106

3 Beatrice doesn't like what she hears
Beatrice doesn't like the idea that people think she's so proud and scornful. She decides to be extra-nice to Benedick — she even hopes he'll marry her. Lines 107-116

Scene Two — Don John Throws a Spanner in the Works

1 Benedick seems to be in love
Don Pedro, Leonato, Claudio and Benedick are discussing Don Pedro's travel plans. Don Pedro wants to take Benedick on his journey to cheer things up. Benedick isn't feeling that cheery. Claudio says maybe it's because he's in love. Benedick denies it and asks to talk to Leonato in private. Don Pedro and Claudio think he's going to ask to marry Beatrice. Lines 1-69

2 Don John gives Claudio something to fret about
Don John comes along. He says he's got something important to tell Claudio — Hero's having an affair. Claudio's easily taken in by the lies. He and Don Pedro agree to meet up with Don John later, so he can prove what he's said is true. Lines 70-123

I love Hero.

She's having an affair.

I hate Hero.

Claudio's supposed to be in love with Hero. It's a pretty **shallow** sort of love if he'll believe Don John's nonsense so easily.

Don John makes me feel like hissing...

There certainly is a lot of talking in this play. They're constantly rabbiting on. I suppose if they didn't it wouldn't be much of a play — more a bunch of people standing around looking moody.

ACT 3 SCENES 3, 4 & 5

What Happens in Act Three

Just when the audience is getting <u>snoozy</u> and <u>restless</u> and thinking about <u>interval ice-creams</u>, <u>Dogberry</u> comes along in Scene Three, spouting nonsense, and wakes them all up.

Scene Three — The <u>Watch Make an Arrest</u>

1 The Watch prepare to do the nightly rounds
Dogberry and Verges give the Watch their instructions for the evening. Dogberry uses a lot of impressive words, but he doesn't know what most of them mean. Lines 1-92

2 The Watch learn about Borachio's trick
Borachio tells Conrade he got 1000 gold ducats from Don John for the trick on Claudio. It all went as planned. Margaret said goodnight to Borachio at Hero's window. Don Pedro and Claudio, who were hiding in the orchard with Don John, believed Margaret was Hero. Don Pedro and Claudio are convinced Hero's having an affair and Claudio's going to break the news at the wedding in the morning. The Watch hear everything. They arrest Conrade and Borachio and take them down to the cells. Line 93-174

Scene Four — <u>Girly Chat Before the Wedding</u>

1 Hero's got some lovely new clothes
Margaret thinks Hero's going to look gorgeous. Hero's got the feeling something bad's going to happen. Margaret tries to cheer her up with smutty jokes. Lines 1-36

2 Beatrice comes to see Hero
Margaret turns her attention to teasing Beatrice about being in love with Benedick. Lines 37-88

3 Ursula says it's time to go to the wedding
Hero rushes inside to dress. Lines 89-93

Scene Five — <u>Dogberry Tries to Explain the Plot</u>

Dogberry and Verges try to explain the plot to Leonato
Leonato's in a hurry to get to the wedding. He can't be bothered with Dogberry and Verges and their long-winded explanation, so he sends them packing.

<u>Dogberry can't explain the plot — maybe he's lost it...</u>

If you're feeling almost as <u>muddled</u> about what's going on as Dogberry at this point don't get your knickers in a twist about it. Keep reading through the section and eventually everything will <u>click</u>.

What Happens in Act Four

Act Four isn't as long as the other acts, but it's <u>BIG</u> on drama. Don John's plotting has exactly the effect he wanted — everyone's angry and upset. I can just picture him <u>sniggering</u> behind his hand.

Scene One — The Big Wedding Ends in Tears

1 Everyone's at the big wedding party

Friar Francis begins the wedding ceremony. Claudio says he doesn't want to get married. The Friar's confused and carries on. Claudio challenges Leonato — he asks whether Hero's really a virgin. Leonato insists she is. Hero and Leonato argue against Claudio, but Leonato starts to believe Claudio and Don Pedro. Hero faints. Don Pedro, Don John and Claudio leave. Lines 1-112

I'm not marrying that brazen hussy.

I wish you would. She's heavier than she looks.

This isn't going too well. I wonder if I'll still be asked in for a sherry.

2 Leonato goes crazy

Beatrice tries to bring Hero round. Leonato's convinced Hero's in the wrong now. Benedick tries to calm him down. Beatrice insists Hero's innocent, and so does the Friar. Friar Francis tells Leonato that the best thing to do is pretend Hero's dead, and let the dust settle. In the meantime they can prove Hero's innocent and Claudio will be so upset that he'll start to think more kindly of Hero again. Leonato agrees and goes off with the Friar and Hero. Lines 113-252

Leonato's ready to <u>believe the worst</u> — it's a good job Hero's friends stand up for her.

3 Beatrice sets Benedick a lover's challenge

Beatrice is sure Hero's innocent — so's Benedick. Beatrice says she would owe a lot to the man who proved Hero's innocence. Benedick blurts out that he loves Beatrice. Beatrice gives him riddling replies but finally admits she loves him too. She asks Benedick to kill Claudio. He says no, and Beatrice goes off on one, wishing she was a man so she could kill Claudio herself. Benedick keeps trying to interrupt. When he finally gets a word in edgeways he says he'll challenge Claudio to a duel. Lines 253-334

Scene Two — Borachio is Interrogated

After all the emotion in Scene One you need a bit of <u>Dogberry</u> to cheer you up...

It's a plot. I'll tell Leonato — you bring the prisoners.

We'd rather come with you.

Dogberry, Verges and the Sexton interview the prisoners

Dogberry, Verges and the Sexton question Borachio and Conrade. With his funny way of talking Dogberry keeps confusing things, but the Sexton, who's a few watts brighter than Dogberry, realises what's going on and rushes away to see Leonato. Dogberry handcuffs the prisoners and follows on behind. Lines 1-84

Borachio — doesn't he play for Juventus...

Scene One is <u>so Eastenders</u> — a ruined wedding, Beatrice in a raging fury and Benedick storming off ready to fight Claudio. I bet if Shakespeare was alive nowadays the <u>BBC</u> would give him a job.

What Happens in Act Five

Roll up your sleeves, pull up your socks and put your hair in a bun — it's time for <u>Act Five</u>. The <u>last</u> in the play. Which is good or bad depending on how much you're <u>enjoying it</u>.

Scene One — Don John's Trick is <u>Exposed</u>

1 Antonio's dead worried about Leonato
Leonato's really upset about Hero's disgrace. Antonio worries that he'll make himself ill, but Leonato tells Antonio to leave him alone. Leonato's convinced that Hero's innocent now, and tells Antonio that's what he thinks. Lines 1-44

2 Leonato rows with Claudio
Leonato rants and raves at Don Pedro and Claudio about how they've got it all wrong about Hero. He almost gets into a fight with Claudio. Don Pedro is still convinced Hero was having an affair. Antonio and Leonato storm out.
Lines 45-109

I'm going to beat you to a pulp.

Yeah, whatever. How's Beatrice?

3 Benedick challenges Claudio
Benedick turns up looking pale and angry. He challenges Claudio to a duel. Claudio and Don Pedro reply with a lot of silly teasing about Beatrice and Benedick. Benedick leaves, saying he wants no more to do with Don Pedro and will definitely fight Claudio. As he leaves he mentions that Don John has done a runner and it looks just a tad suspicious. Lines 110-190

4 Borachio owns up
Claudio carries on mucking about, but Don Pedro turns serious. He realises Benedick wouldn't get so cross about nothing — they've most probably been tricked by Don John. Dogberry and Verges bring in Borachio. Don Pedro asks Borachio why he's under arrest. Borachio admits everything — that Don John persuaded him to do the trick, and that the woman Don Pedro and Claudio saw at Hero's bedroom window was actually Margaret dressed in Hero's clothes. Don Pedro and Claudio are dead upset – they think they've killed Hero with their false accusations.
Lines 191-252

You numbskull — you still don't get it. We've been tricked.

Oops.

5 Leonato plays a new trick
Leonato's heard the news about the trick from the Sexton. He charges in, yelling at Borachio, Don Pedro and Claudio. He tells Claudio to do three things to make up for his treating Hero so badly: clear her name with the people of Messina; write an epitaph for her tomb; and marry Antonio's daughter, who looks just like Hero… Claudio agrees to do all three. Leonato thanks Dogberry and goes to question Margaret, taking Borachio with him. Claudio says he's going to spend the night in mourning at Hero's tomb.
Lines 253-326

Antonio <u>hasn't got a daughter</u>. This is Leonato's trick — he's going to bring Hero to the new wedding in disguise.

What Happens in Act Five

Scene Two and Scene Three are <u>weirdly different</u>. <u>Scene Two</u> is a <u>jolly, flirty love scene</u> with Beatrice and Benedick. Straight after it you get <u>Scene Three</u> which is all very <u>dark</u> and <u>sombre</u> with Claudio grieving for Hero, who he thinks is dead.

Scene 2 — Beatrice and Benedick Get Smoochy

1 Benedick's waiting to see Beatrice
Benedick asks Margaret to go and get Beatrice. Left on his own, he muses on how he's tried to write poems for Beatrice, but not managed it. Lines 1-40

2 Benedick flirts with Beatrice
Benedick tries to charm and flatter Beatrice but she responds with more jokes than kisses. Beatrice tells Benedick that Hero is still very upset, and that she's not feeling too great either. Lines 41-87

3 Ursula says Hero's proved innocent
Ursula comes rushing in to tell Beatrice and Benedick that Hero's innocence has finally been proved. They all go to Leonato's house to find out more. Lines 88-96

<u>Beatrice</u> doesn't think Benedick and her are the soppy type:

Thou and I are too wise to woo peaceably.
Line 67

I love you, Beatrice.

Oh right, me too. Anyway, this horse goes into a bar...

Scene 3 — Claudio Grieves for Hero

This scene's very <u>calm</u> compared to the rest of the play. It gives the audience a little <u>break</u> before the big finale.

So long Hero!
It's all my fault
You're dead and buried
In the family vault.

It's a bit late now, buster.
Have you got any biscuits?

1 Claudio visits Hero's tomb
In the middle of the night Claudio arrives at the family tomb belonging to Leonato. Claudio thinks Hero is buried here and hangs the epitaph on the tomb as he agreed with Leonato. Balthasar sings a sad mourning song for Hero. Claudio says he will come and do the same ritual every year to show how sorry he is for Hero's death. Lines 1-23

2 Dawn breaks and the mood gets brighter
As dawn breaks Don Pedro and Claudio go off to change ready for the new wedding. Lines 24-33

Beatrice and Benedick sitting in a tree...

Scene Three is definitely the <u>least funny</u> scene in the play. Even though the audience all know that Hero isn't really dead it's still quite <u>sad</u>. There are <u>no jokes</u>, <u>no tricks</u> and <u>no flirting</u>. It's set at <u>night</u> and most of the rest of the play's set in daytime. Cheer up though, the next scene's <u>jolly</u>...

What Happens in Act Five

Finally Hero has her wedding...

Scene 4 — The Wedding Scene (at last)

1 It's the morning of the wedding

The Friar, Leonato, Antonio and Benedick are chatting — they're all relieved everything has turned out so well. Leonato sends Beatrice, Hero, Ursula and Margaret to wait indoors. He tells them to wear their veils when they come back out. Antonio is going to give Hero away, pretending she's his daughter. Lines 1-17

2 Benedick makes a special request

Benedick asks Leonato for permission to marry Beatrice. Leonato agrees, and the Friar says he can marry them at the same time as Hero and Claudio. Lines 18-33

3 The groom arrives

Leonato welcomes Don Pedro and Claudio. Antonio goes to fetch the women. He presents Hero to Claudio. Claudio asks her to lift the veil, but Leonato says she won't till Claudio's sworn to marry her. He swears it and Hero lifts the veil. She insists she was innocent all along. Lines 34-71

You lovely ladies pop inside and put your veils on.

A veil really suits you, Margaret.

Same to you, Ursula.

Leonato wants to <u>make</u> <u>sure</u> Claudio marries Hero this time.

The Friar's here, the church is booked and the reception's paid for. Let's get married, baby.

That's not very romantic — no I won't. Actually, yes I will.

We don't get to actually <u>see</u> the weddings — the play ends with dancing.

4 Benedick asks Beatrice to marry him

Benedick and Beatrice almost talk themselves out of getting married, but finally agree to it. Lines 72-97

5 They all live happily ever after...

Benedick calls for music — he wants everyone to dance and enjoy themselves before the ceremony. At the last minute a messenger comes with news that Don John's been arrested, but Benedick asks Don Pedro to forget about him till tomorrow. Everyone dances, and the play comes to an end. Lines 98-126

I'm moved to tears — really I am...

So there you have it — <u>everything works out in the end</u>. Claudio and Hero are together, Benedick and Beatrice are together and they all dance off into the sunset. Isn't it just <u>lovely</u>...

Revision Summary

Right now I'm finding it fairly hard to believe, but Much Ado About Nothing *is one of the shorter Shakespeare plays. Just because it's short(ish) doesn't make it easy to learn the story. You've got to follow all those tricks and counter-tricks so you know what's going on and who knows what. These questions should help you test whether you're getting on top of things or not. You only really know the story when you can answer them all without looking back at the section.*

1) Which two characters aren't very keen on love and marriage at the beginning?

2) Write down as many points as you can explaining why Claudio and Hero's relationship is very different from Beatrice and Benedick's.

3) Which character likes making crude, smutty jokes?

4) Write down the names of five posh characters in *Much Ado*.

5) Explain how girls and women were supposed to behave in Shakespeare's day.

6) Describe five tricks that the characters play on each other in *Much Ado*.

7) Who was Don Pedro fighting a war against?

8) Who's in love with Hero at the beginning of the play?

9) Who does Antonio *think* is in love with Hero?

10) Who tells Don John about the plans for Hero and Claudio to get married?

11) Why is Benedick so upset by what Beatrice says to him at the dance?

12) What does Don John tell Claudio at the dance?

13) Who comes up with the plan to get Beatrice and Benedick together?

14) Describe Don John's plan for splitting up Claudio and Hero.

15) Who fools Benedick in the garden?

16) Who tricks Beatrice? What does the trick make her believe?

17) What does Claudio tease Benedick about in Act 3, Scene 2?

18) Who tells Claudio that Hero's been unfaithful?

19) Why does the Watch arrest Borachio?

20) Why doesn't Leonato listen when Dogberry tries to explain the plot?

21) Who suggests to Leonato that they should pretend Hero's dead after the failed wedding?

22) Who asks Benedick to kill Claudio?

23) Who finally works out Don John's trick?

24) What three things does Leonato ask Claudio to do in Act 5, Scene 1.

25) What does Claudio promise he will do every year at Hero's tomb?

26) Why does Leonato tell Hero to wear a veil for the wedding?

27) Name everyone who's agreed to get married at the end of the play.

Well, all's well that ends well.

Shut up, you idiot, that's the wrong play.

Section 4 — Understanding The Story

Three Steps for an Essay

So you've had a good look at the <u>play</u>. In this section we'll look at the kind of <u>essay</u> you'll have to write, and some good tips for getting really <u>good marks</u> in the test.

Three Steps to Exam Success

These three steps are a <u>little treasure</u> for answering exam questions. And they work for <u>any kind</u> of Shakespeare question — bargain.

1) Read the question and <u>underline</u> the important bits.

2) Go through the set scenes and look for <u>examples</u> you could use in your answer.

3) Do a quick <u>plan</u> for your essay. Look back at this when you're writing so you don't run out of ideas.

See pages 32-33 for more about planning.

The Question Will Look Like This

Whichever question type you get, the <u>basic layout</u> will look like this:

Much Ado About Nothing

Act 1 Scene 1, lines 143-180
Act 4 Scene 1, lines 21-107

In these scenes, Claudio tells Benedick he loves Hero, then accuses Hero of being unfaithful.

How do these scenes show different sides of Claudio's character?

Support your ideas by referring to both of the extracts which are printed on the following pages.

18 marks

There might be a bit like this to introduce the <u>topic</u> of the question.

This bit tells you which <u>parts of the play</u> the question is about. It'll be about half the set scenes (printed on pages **48-55** of this book).

This basically means "keep looking at the scenes and include loads of <u>quotes</u>".

This is the really important bit — the actual <u>question</u>. It's <u>important</u> that you read this carefully, so that you fully understand what you're being asked.

Steps? I thought they'd split up...

Although there are a few different types of question (see Section 6), they all pretty much follow the <u>same format</u> as the one on this page. So get familiar with it and you'll know what to expect.

Using Quotes

For every point you make, you have to back it up by using a quote. Quotes prove your points — if you don't use them, you've got no proof that you're not just making it up.

Keep the Quotes Short

Keep quotes short and to the point — a couple of lines is usually enough.

e.g.

Claudio unfairly accuses Hero of being unfaithful, in front of all the wedding guests. At this point we see a cruel, harsh side to his character:

"She knows the heat of a luxurious bed:
Her blush is guiltiness, not modesty."

Act 4, Scene 1, 39-40

Start a new paragraph.

Copy down the exact words.

Say where the quote comes from. Give the act, scene, and line numbers.

If the quote's less than a line you don't need to put it in a separate paragraph or say where the quote's from, but you do need to put it in speech marks.

Now do you see what I mean?

Claudio insults Hero on a number of occasions. At one point he tells her father Leonato that she is a "rotten orange".

Explain Why the Quote is Relevant

1) Remember to make it really clear why you've included the quotes — don't just stick them in and expect the examiner to see the point you're making.

e.g.

Early on in the play, Claudio seems to be totally in love with Hero. He tells Benedick he thinks Hero is "the sweetest lady that ever I looked on". However, Claudio is very easily tricked into believing that she is an "approved wanton". This suggests he is very gullible and quick to change his mind.

These quotes are good because they show something about Claudio's character, which is what the question's about.

2) Quote different characters — this makes your answer more interesting. E.g. You could include Don Pedro's description of Claudio as "my dear friend".

3) Remember though that characters will have particular reasons for saying certain things — don't assume they're being totally honest and fair.

Status Quote — the studious rock band...

So the main points about quoting are: 1) Keep 'em short. 2) Explain how they answer the question. This'll make sure the quotes really add something to your answer.

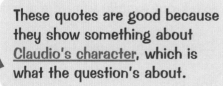

Section 5 — Writing an Essay

Planning and Structure

If you <u>plan</u> your essay first, you'll have <u>more</u> chance of getting loads of <u>marks</u>.

You Need a Beginning, a Middle and an End

A good essay has a <u>beginning</u>,
a <u>middle</u> and an <u>end</u>.
Just like a good story.

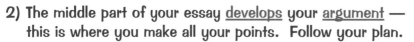

Just like me then.

1) The <u>hardest</u> part is <u>beginning</u> your essay. The <u>first sentence</u> has to start <u>answering</u> the question, and tell the examiner that your essay is going to be good. All that from <u>one</u> sentence — so you'd better start <u>practising</u>.

2) The middle part of your essay <u>develops</u> your <u>argument</u> — this is where you make all your points. Follow your plan.

3) The end <u>sums up</u> the points you've made and <u>rounds</u> the essay <u>off</u> nicely.

Before you Write, Make a Plan

I wish I was organised...

Planning means <u>organising</u> your material to help you write a clear answer that makes sense. A good plan turns that <u>heap of ideas</u> in your head into an <u>argument</u> supported by <u>points</u>.

Planning might seem a <u>pain</u> to do, but if you do it, you'll be <u>less</u> likely to get <u>lost</u> halfway through the essay.

Five Steps to Planning a Good Essay

1) Work out <u>exactly</u> what the question is asking you to do. Find the <u>key words</u> and <u>underline</u> them.

2) Read the <u>set scenes</u> — highlight <u>quotations</u> you could use.

3) Jot down your <u>ideas</u> — from the set scenes they <u>give</u> you, and from your <u>knowledge</u> of the <u>rest</u> of the play — and then put them into an <u>order</u>.

4) Decide what your <u>opinion</u> is, and how you can <u>use</u> your points to <u>support</u> it — to form an <u>argument</u>. Put your <u>best</u> point <u>first</u>.

5) Don't stick to your plan <u>rigidly</u>. If you think of any more <u>good ideas</u> once you've started writing, then try to fit them in.

It's the beginning of the end...

If you're not sure what your <u>opinion</u> is, state the arguments <u>for and against</u>, and give evidence to support each viewpoint. Answer the question by <u>comparing</u> the views on <u>each side</u>.

Planning and Structure

Here's an example of how you could make a plan for a question on Much Ado About Nothing.

Work out What the Question is Asking

e.g.

Act 1 Scene 1, lines 152-219 and Act 2 Scene 3, lines 81-225

Describe how Benedick's attitude to love and marriage seems to change in these scenes.

Support your ideas by referring to the scenes.

1) Start by underlining the most important words in the question.
For this one you'd underline "Benedick", "love" and "marriage".

2) Once you've got the question in your head, go through the scenes and pick out sections of the scenes that look like they'll help your answer.

> Because I will not do them the wrong to mistrust any, I will do myself the right to trust none: and the fine is, for the which I may go the finer, I will live a bachelor.
> Act 1, Scene 1, 217-219

3) Go through the scenes again and check for things you might have missed — it looks really good if you can find points that are relevant but not obvious.

Making Your Plan

Next jot down a plan for your essay. Don't bother writing in proper English in your plan — just get your ideas down.

This essay's all about Benedick. Make notes on everything you think is relevant from the scene — concentrate on the bits where Benedick is speaking.

Decide on the best order to write about your points in.

Write down any comments you've got on what happens.

Scribble down good quotes to back it all up.

> *Describe how Benedick's attitude to love and marriage seems to change in these scenes.*
>
> 1. *Attitude to Claudio* Amazed how quickly he's changed. Makes fun out of Claudio for being in love with Hero — "Leonato's short daughter".
>
> 3. ~~2.~~ *Quick to believe Beatrice is in love with him* First reaction to news Beatrice is in love with him is surprise — "Is't possible?" — but by end of scene totally believes it. Has changed just as quickly as Claudio — a bit ironic.
>
> 2. ~~3.~~ *At beginning not keen on marriage* Says he doesn't trust women to be faithful to him. Determined to "live a bachelor".

My essay blossomed — I plant it well...

Don't just launch straight in — take the time to plan. Once you've jotted some ideas down, you'll realise you have more to say than you thought — so there's less reason to panic. And let's face it, a structured essay will get more marks than one that goes all over the place...

Writing Your Answer

Once you've got a plan, you're <u>ready</u> to start writing.
Make your points as <u>clearly</u> as you can so the examiner knows what you're on about.

Write a Simple Opening Paragraph

Start by using the exact <u>words of the task</u> in your introduction.
This shows you've <u>understood</u> the question.

Your introduction <u>doesn't</u> have to be <u>long</u> at all. It's just there to show what your <u>basic answer</u> to the task is. In the rest of the paragraphs you'll need to go into <u>detail</u>.

 e.g.

> _Describe how Benedick's attitude to love and marriage seems to change in these scenes._
>
> In the first scene, Benedick starts off sounding very scornful of <u>love and marriage</u>. By the end, his <u>attitude</u> is very different and he is hoping for love and marriage himself.
>
> At first, Benedick laughs at the idea of being in love ...

The opening sentences use words from the <u>question</u>.

Once you've written your opening paragraph, just follow the order of your <u>plan</u> to write the rest of your essay.

Make Your Answer Interesting

1) Use <u>interesting</u> words — the examiner will get <u>bored</u> if you <u>overuse</u> dull words and phrases like "nice" and "I think". Try using words like "<u>fascinating</u>" and phrases like "<u>in my opinion</u>".

2) Keep your style <u>formal</u> — write in full sentences and don't use slang words. This makes your argument more <u>convincing</u> and gets you even more <u>marks</u>.

3) If you think a passage is "poetic", "realistic" etc., remember to explain <u>exactly why</u> — with examples. <u>Don't</u> assume it's <u>obvious</u> to the examiner.

Boring!

It was a nice day, and everyone had a nice time.

Keep bearing in mind the <u>words</u> used in the <u>question</u>. Using them in your essay will show you're <u>keeping to the task</u> and not getting lost.

Allow me to introduce my lovely essay...

Your intro really doesn't need to be anything mindblowing. Just a couple of sentences to show you've <u>understood</u> the question and get your answer started. Then you start moving onto more <u>detailed</u> points in the rest of your answer, with some nice tasty <u>quotes</u> to back them up.

Concluding and Checking for Errors

Once you've made <u>all</u> your points, you need to <u>sum up</u> your answer and <u>check</u> it through.

Write a Conclusion to Sum Up Your Key Points

The conclusion to my speech will be very concise — barely half an hour...

1) Start a new <u>paragraph</u> for your conclusion.

2) Sum up the <u>main points</u> of your essay <u>briefly</u>. This makes it clear how you've <u>answered</u> the question.

3) Don't go on and on, though. It's best if your conclusion is just a <u>couple of sentences</u>.

Go Over Your Essay When You've Finished

1) Try to <u>leave time</u> at the end to <u>read through</u> your essay quickly. Check that it <u>makes sense</u>, that you haven't got any facts wrong, and that it says what you <u>want</u> it to say.

How many more times do I have to go over it?

2) Check the <u>grammar</u>, <u>spelling</u> and <u>punctuation</u>. If you find a <u>mistake</u>, put <u>brackets</u> round it, cross it out <u>neatly</u> with two lines through it and write the <u>correction</u> above.

Nothing
Much Ado About (~~Nowt~~)

Don't <u>scribble</u> or put <u>whitener</u> on mistakes — it looks <u>messy</u> and you'll <u>lose marks</u>.

3) If you've written something which isn't <u>clear</u>, put an <u>asterisk</u> * at the end of the sentence. Put another asterisk in the <u>margin</u>, and write what you <u>mean</u> in the margin.

He says Hero had an affair. | Don John lies to Claudio.

Don't Panic if You Realise You've Gone Wrong

If you realise you've <u>forgotten</u> something really <u>obvious</u> and <u>easy</u>, then write a <u>note</u> about it at the bottom of the <u>final</u> page, to tell the examiner. If there's time, write an extra <u>paragraph</u>. You'll pick up marks for <u>noticing</u> your mistake.

<u>Don't give up</u> if you're running out of <u>time</u> — even if you only have <u>five minutes</u> left, that's still time to pick up <u>extra marks</u>.

Check, check, check — I must be rich...

You've almost <u>finished</u>. Keep your conclusions <u>to the point</u>, and <u>check</u> your essay so you don't <u>throw away</u> marks on <u>silly mistakes</u>. Keep a <u>clear head</u> right up to the end — then it's <u>teatime</u>.

Revision Summary

I like to think of it as the 5 Ps — Planning Prevents Pitifully Poor Performance. Actually, I think it's a bit more positive than that — Planning Provides Practically Perfect Performance. The main point is Planning Planning Planning Planning Planning. Anyway, that's enough Ps for now. On with the revision summary — you only know the answers when you don't have to flick back.

1) Name three useful things you should do before you start writing an answer to an exam question.

2) Why is it important to use lots of quotes in your essay?

3) What three bits of information do you have to give after any quote that's more than a line long?

4) What punctuation marks do you use on quotes that are shorter than one line?

5) What should you explain about every quote you use?

6) What are the three vital ingredients of a good essay?
   a) Spelling, handwriting and punctuation.
   b) Great ideas, brilliant ideas and fantastic ideas.
   c) A beginning, a middle and an end.

7) What's the big advantage of making a plan for an essay question?

8) If you have a great idea when you're writing your essay which wasn't on your original plan, is it OK to fit it into your essay anyway?

9) How important is it to write your plan in proper English?

10) What do you have to do with the first sentence of the answer?
   a) Give a general answer to the question.
   b) Make your best point straightaway.
   c) Put in a really interesting quote.

11) Should you use mostly formal language or mostly slang in your answer?

12) How long should your closing paragraph be?
   a) About half a page.
   b) As long as a piece of string.
   c) As short as possible but including all the main points from the essay.

13) Write down four things you should check for when you read through your essay at the end.

14) How do you correct a spelling mistake?

15) What should you do if you'd written something which isn't clear?

How do you spell "clueless"?

Questions About a Character

You might be asked a question about a particular <u>character</u> in Much Ado About Nothing.

Character Questions are Fairly Simple

Questions about a character will often ask you <u>what the scenes show</u> about that person.

> **e.g.** Act 1 Scene 3 and Act 2 Scene 2
> In these scenes we learn about Don John's character.
> **How is Don John shown to be an unpleasant character?**
> *Support your ideas by referring to the scenes.*

Start by <u>underlining</u> the most <u>important</u> words in the question —
you can write on the exam paper.

> <u>How</u> is Don John shown to be an <u>unpleasant</u> character?

You have to explain how Shakespeare lets the audience know Don John's a baddie.

These are the most important words. They tell you what to write about.

Look at what Characters Say about Each Other

1) The characters aren't just <u>gossiping</u> when they talk about each other
— Shakespeare often gives the audience <u>messages</u> about characters through what <u>other characters</u> say about them.

2) E.g. When Claudio comes in half way through Act 1 Scene 1, we already know he's a <u>great fighter</u> and he's <u>noble</u>, because the messenger has talked about it. Shakespeare wants us to be <u>on Claudio's side</u> right through the play — even when he treats Hero like rubbish.

Ooh, that Claudio's not 'alf handy with his sword...

3) If the characters told us about <u>themselves</u> then we'd think they were <u>showing off</u> — and we wouldn't believe them. And if all the important stuff, like Claudio's fights, were <u>acted out</u> in the play, it would go on for ages. Instead, Shakespeare uses a <u>short cut</u> — someone tells us about it.

That Don John, eh? What a character...

These questions shouldn't ask you anything <u>unexpected</u> — you should know about the characters and their odd little ways before the exam. Try to be really <u>thorough</u> and there'll be no hiccups.

| CHARACTER QUESTIONS | # *Characters — The Bigger Picture* |

If you're asked to write about a <u>character</u> there are <u>a few things</u> you can do to get <u>more marks</u> — it's a question of looking for the <u>less obvious</u> things.

Think About what Motivates the Characters

1) <u>Motivation</u> means the <u>reasons</u> a character has for acting as they do.

2) The characters in Much Ado are all after <u>different things</u>.
Some people are driven by <u>good intentions</u>, some by <u>bad intentions</u>.
Some of them do things for <u>themselves</u>, some do things for <u>others</u>.

3) Show that you understand what <u>motivates</u> the character you're writing about.
Find a good <u>quote</u> and say what it tells you about the character:

When Don John first hears of the wedding plans, he immediately asks Borachio if it will give him "any model to build mischief on". This shows that he is motivated purely by the thought of causing trouble, rather than any sense of right or wrong.

Some People Never Change

Shakespeare's <u>audience</u> expected certain characters to behave in certain ways.

> Don John will always be a <u>baddie</u> — the audience know this because he's Don Pedro's <u>illegitimate brother</u> (see page 14). He even calls himself "a plain-dealing villain" in Act 1 Scene 3, line 28.

> <u>Hero's</u> another example. She <u>doesn't get angry</u> with Claudio in Act 4 Scene 1 because she's a respectful young lady who does what men <u>expect</u> her to do (see page 11). The play wouldn't work if she <u>changed</u> right at the end.

Remember, people in Shakespeare's time had <u>different ideas</u> than us about what was <u>normal</u>.

Look Out for Opposites

1) <u>Claudio and Hero</u> are young, innocent and <u>happy to be in love</u> — but the other young couple, <u>Beatrice and Benedick</u> spend loads of time <u>arguing</u>, even though we know they'll get together in the end. The play would be really dull if <u>all</u> the characters went <u>soppy</u> over love.

2) <u>Don Pedro and Don John</u> are brothers. But Don Pedro is <u>wise</u> and <u>noble</u> — whereas Don John is <u>bad</u> through and through. We need Don John to liven things up a bit.

> You need to know the <u>whole play</u> to find out about this stuff — if you only know your set scenes it'll be much harder to write about how you react to a certain character.

Bill Shakes-beer — the nervous pub landlord...

So that's one type of exam question. Writing about characters is probably the <u>simplest</u> of the four kinds of question we'll look at. On the next two pages we'll look at writing about language.

How Language Is Used

If you're asked about Shakespeare's "use of language", it just means <u>what words he uses</u>.

Language Can Tell us About Characters

The kind of words each character uses affects our <u>impression</u> of them.

1) <u>Benedick</u> and <u>Beatrice</u> use clever <u>word play</u> to try and put each other down. This shows that they are <u>proud</u> and <u>witty</u>.

Then find the remainder...

> BENEDICK: Well, you are a rare parrot-teacher.
> BEATRICE: A bird of my tongue is better than a beast of yours.
> BENEDICK: I would my horse had the speed of your tongue.
> Act 1, Scene 1, 124-126

2) The <u>rude joke</u> that <u>Margaret</u> makes in Act 3 Scene 4 — that Hero's heart will be heavier "by the weight of a man" — suggests that Margaret's a bit <u>vulgar</u>.

3) <u>Hero's</u> reaction to the joke — "art not ashamed?" — shows that she's <u>innocent</u> and <u>easily shocked</u>.

Language can be Used to Create Comedy

1) A lot of the comedy comes from the <u>Watch</u>, when they keep <u>getting their words wrong</u>.

2) E.g. Dogberry tries to sound very <u>important</u>, to try to sound like he knows what he's doing. But the silly long words he uses just make him look pretty <u>stupid</u>.

> DOGBERRY: Is our whole dissembly appeared?
> VERGES: Oh a stool and a cushion for the sexton.
> SEXTON: Which be the malefactors?
> DOGBERRY: Marry that am I, and my partner.
> Act 4, Scene 2, 1-4

He means "assembly", not "dissembly".

Here he accidentally says he's a criminal ("malefactor" means "wrongdoer").

3) The comic language of the Watch <u>contrasts</u> with the more <u>serious</u>, <u>sinister</u> language of Don John and his mates. It's important because it <u>lightens the mood</u> — Much Ado About Nothing is a comedy, after all.

As long as it's not in Swedish, you'll be fine...

Studying Shakespeare is really <u>all about</u> looking at what language he uses. So if you get a question that asks you specifically about his <u>choice of words</u>, there should be <u>plenty</u> you can write about.

LANGUAGE QUESTIONS

How Language Creates Mood

"Mood" or "atmosphere" means the <u>feel</u> of a scene — whether it's tense, funny, exciting or whatever. You might be asked about <u>how language is used</u> to create a particular <u>mood</u>.

Say what Effect the Words Create

 Act 4 Scene 1, lines 1-141 and Act 5 Scene 3, whole scene
How does Shakespeare's use of language create a serious mood in these scenes?

Make it serious...
How about some snakes? No...

Use words from the question.

Explain the exact effect of the language.

Say how the language creates the effect you've described.

The mood of Act 4 Scene 1 is particularly serious because of the language Claudio uses towards Hero when he accuses her of not being a virgin. He calls her a "rotten orange" and a "wanton". These words are very insulting and would make Hero feel humiliated in public, especially because it was seen to be very important for a woman to be a virgin before marriage.

The mood becomes even darker when Hero's father turns against her. Leonato says he would rather she was dead than dishonoured: "Hence from her! Let her die." The harshness of this language means that the normally happy feel of the wedding day has been turned into a nightmare for Hero.

Keep the answer focused and to-the-point.

Quote loads.

Look for Mood Changes Within Scenes

It'll add a little <u>extra</u> to your answer if you can identify the place where the mood of a scene <u>changes</u>. For example, if you were writing about Act 4, Scene 1, you could say something like:

Show how the language reflects the change.

When Claudio tells Leonato "you learn me noble thankfulness", the tone is formal but appears to be pleasant, and there is little sign of what is to follow.

However, the mood of the scene changes dramatically when Claudio says he will not marry Hero. Claudio suddenly tells Leonato to "take her back again", before accusing and insulting Hero. From this point onwards the mood is angry and aggressive.

Say where the change in mood happens.

Heaven knows I'm miserable now... but not now...

So there's quite a bit you can write about for these questions to please the examiner. They give you the opportunity to really go to town and show off your <u>understanding</u> of the language.

Writing About a Theme

Theme questions sound more tricky than they really are. They're generally just asking how the play puts across a particular message or idea.

Work Out What the Question is Asking

Theme questions are often worded like this:

> **Act 4 Scene 1, lines 108-198 and Act 5 Scene 1, lines 45-105**
>
> In these scenes, Leonato and Antonio are devastated by accusations about Hero.
>
> **How do these extracts show the importance of honour and reputation?**
>
> *Support your ideas by referring to the scenes.*

Don't panic if the question seems complicated.

Read it carefully, and you'll realise it's actually pretty simple.

> You could rephrase this as:
> "These bits of the play show that honour and reputation are important. How do they do this?"

Theme Questions Aren't as Hard as They Look

1) Read through the scenes with the question in mind, and some points should pretty much leap out at you and give you the basis for a good answer.
   For example, for the question above, this quote from Leonato would be useful:

> Why doth not every earthly thing
> Cry shame upon her? Could she here deny
> The story that is printed in her blood?
> Do not live, Hero, do not ope thine eyes:
> For did I think thou wouldst not quickly die,
> Thought I thy spirits were stronger than thy shames,
> Myself would on the rearward of approaches
> Strike at thy life.
>
> Act 4, Scene 1, 118-125

> This is the worst thing that's happened since Messina got relegated.

2) Once you've found a good extract like this, just say how it relates to the question. Don't forget to stick in some good quotes to back up your points:

> *Leonato is so concerned about losing his good reputation that he would rather Hero dies than for the stories about her to become known. He harshly tells her, "do not ope thine eyes", without even giving her the chance to deny the accusations.*

I don't like extracts — they remind me of dentists...

Questions about themes generally tell you an opinion, then ask you to prove that it's true. Which makes it easy really — no faffing about deciding what to argue, just find some good evidence.

Themes You Might be Asked About

Here's a few more things you can do if you get a question about a <u>theme</u> or <u>issue</u> in Much Ado.

There are <u>Several Themes</u> in Much Ado

If you do get a <u>theme question</u>, it's likely to be about one of:

- honour and reputation
- tricks and disguises
- love and marriage
- evil
- innocence
- wit

It's worth having a think about these themes and working out <u>what you'd write</u> about them. Have a look at pages 17-19 for more about the <u>themes</u> in Much Ado.

Look for the <u>Less Obvious</u> Bits

1) There will usually be plenty of fairly <u>obvious points</u> you can use in your answer to a theme question (like the stuff on the previous page).

2) But if you want to get really <u>great marks</u>, you'll need to go into a bit more <u>detail</u>. Try to write something that answers the question in a way that's <u>not</u> immediately obvious.

> *Leonato's angry speech in Act 5 Scene 1 suggests that he believes honour is more important than youth and physical strength. He says that despite his "grey hairs and bruise of many days", he is still prepared to fight Claudio. He seems confident that his sense of honour alone will help him win, despite Claudio's "bloom of lustihood".*

3) It's especially important that you give <u>evidence</u> for these kinds of points. The examiner might not have thought of this, so it's <u>vital</u> you back it up with good <u>quotations</u>.

Exhibit A

4) Don't go <u>over the top</u> trying to write blindingly original stuff — make sure you don't miss out the <u>clear-cut</u> points that'll give you easy marks. But if you can stick in just <u>one or two</u> more unexpected, well-explained points into your plan, along with the easier stuff, they'll make your answer really <u>stand out</u>.

Make sure you stick to the question — it's easy to go off the point when you're trying to come up with a really original answer.

Where do topics go to have fun? A theme park...

You'll <u>never</u> get a question that asks you something unexpected, like "Explore how the play suggests that life is all about eating squid". It'll always be a fairly <u>obvious</u> theme, so don't worry.

Directing a Scene

The <u>fourth</u> type of exam question you might get asks you to imagine you're a <u>director</u> —
the person who's <u>in charge</u> of the performance of the play.

As a Director you can be Creative

If you get a question on how you'd direct a scene, it's a good opportunity to <u>use your imagination</u>.
It's all about how to make the play look and sound great <u>on stage</u>. Here's an example question:

> **Act 3 Scene 3, lines 1-77 and Act 4 Scene 2, whole scene**
>
> Imagine you are a director.
>
> **How would you direct the actors playing Dogberry and Verges in these scenes?**
>
> *Explain your ideas by referring closely to the extracts.*

Don't make the same mistake I did — remember to hire some actors.

Use the Language and Stage Directions

These questions can be a bit <u>scary</u> if you're struggling to think of good ideas.
But there will be plenty of <u>clues</u> in the text which will give you some <u>ideas</u>.

1) <u>Look for LINES that stand out</u>

Find some lines that sound <u>dramatic</u> —
happy, angry, scary, anything emotional.

Then think about <u>how</u> the actor should say
these lines to really give them <u>impact</u>.

2) <u>Look for STAGE DIRECTIONS</u>

These hint at what's happening on
stage — e.g. who's <u>moving</u> where, or
what <u>sounds</u> and <u>lighting</u> there are.

You can <u>interpret</u> these — say <u>how</u>
you'd make them happen.

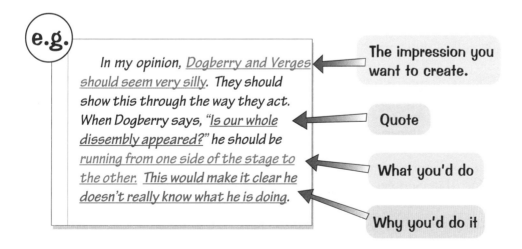

e.g.

In my opinion, <u>Dogberry and Verges should seem very silly</u>. They should show this through the way they act. When Dogberry says, "<u>Is our whole dissembly appeared?</u>" he should be <u>running from one side of the stage to the other</u>. <u>This would make it clear he doesn't really know what he is doing</u>.

The impression you want to create.

Quote

What you'd do

Why you'd do it

Die-rector — threatening a clergyman?

As with the other questions, you <u>don't</u> have to come up with loads of really <u>groundbreaking</u> ideas.
Just give some <u>well-explained suggestions</u> with the odd more detailed point and you're well away.

DIRECTING QUESTIONS | # How the Characters Should Speak

It's fair to say that the <u>most important</u> thing about Shakespeare is the <u>words</u> he uses. So as a director, you have to help the actors get the <u>meaning</u> of these words across to the <u>audience</u>.

Actors can <u>Say Their Lines</u> in Different Ways

1) Have a think about the <u>meaning</u> of the lines, then decide how you can <u>get this across</u> to the <u>audience</u>. It's all to do with <u>tone of voice</u> — e.g. angry, friendly, sarcastic.

2) There's no right or wrong answer. As long as you <u>explain why</u> you think an actor should speak in a certain way, and give some <u>evidence</u> from the play, you <u>can't go wrong</u>.

3) You can even suggest <u>more than one way</u> for the actor to speak a line — the examiner will like this, as it shows you're <u>thinking</u> really hard about the play. Just make sure you give <u>reasons</u> for each suggestion you make.

SPEAK UP!

(e.g.) *When Claudio decides to tell everyone what he believes about Hero, he is probably feeling quite angry and bitter. He could show this by <u>shouting</u> the line, "Out on thee! Seeming!".*

However, it might be better for him to speak <u>very quietly</u> so that the audience <u>has to listen hard</u>. This would add to the tension in the scene.

Give an idea about <u>how</u> the lines should be said.

Give <u>another opinion</u> if you have one.

Always <u>explain</u> why you have a certain idea. This is the <u>most important</u> part of your answer.

You can Create a Sense of <u>Anticipation</u>

1) <u>Anticipation</u> means wanting to know <u>what will happen next</u>. Shakespeare sometimes creates a feeling of anticipation by letting the <u>audience</u> know something the <u>characters don't</u> — this is called <u>dramatic irony</u>.

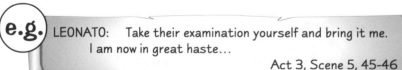

(e.g.) LEONATO: Take their examination yourself and bring it me. I am now in great haste...
Act 3, Scene 5, 45-46

2) Here, Leonato sends Dogberry away when <u>we know</u> he could have <u>stopped</u> Don John's plan against Claudio. This increases the <u>tension</u> before the wedding scene.

3) When writing as a director, you can say how you'd <u>add to the drama</u> of the scene. E.g. For the bit above, Leonato could be walking away from Dogberry as he is speaking.

Shtop! Thish play is not ready yet...

Being a director means giving your own <u>interpretation</u> of the play. Keep thinking about the effect you want to create on the <u>audience</u> — they're what it's all about. And be <u>enthusiastic</u> — it works.

How the Characters Should Act

The director can also create <u>mood</u> for the <u>audience</u> by thinking about how to get the actors to act and move.

Think About how Different Characters will Act

<u>Different characters</u> will act in different ways in a scene. You can <u>compare</u> the way different characters act to show how <u>mood</u> is put across to the audience.

 e.g.

> _Although Claudio is angry, Hero is probably feeling_
> _very humiliated._ When she says, "Is my lord well…"
> she should speak very politely but quietly, _to show_
> _that she can't believe what she is hearing._

Show that you know they <u>don't all feel the same</u>.

Here's your <u>explanation</u> again — really important.

Think about how the characters are <u>feeling</u>, then how to <u>show this</u> in their <u>tone of voice</u>. And remember you can <u>compare</u> different characters and their <u>feelings</u> in the same scene.

Tell the Actors How to Move

They're actors, so make 'em <u>act</u>. Their <u>body language</u> — gestures, posture, movement — has a big effect on how their characters come across, and you can suggest things that aren't in the stage directions. As ever, <u>explain your ideas</u> and stick to the <u>evidence</u> in the play.

e.g.

> _When Claudio calls Hero a "rotten orange", he could_
> _turn his back on her, to show he is dismissing her._
> _However, in my opinion, it would be better if he_
> _really intimidates her by going right up to her to_
> _say this line. He feels he has been treated like a_
> _fool, and this would show how bitter he feels._

Describe the <u>effect</u> you're trying to create.

Use phrases like "<u>in my opinion</u>" — they show it's <u>your idea</u> and you're <u>exploring</u> the play.

<u>Expand</u> on your idea.

If you talk about two <u>different ideas</u> about how to direct a scene, your answer will look better if you <u>link</u> your points together.

<u>Linking words</u> are dead useful. They help you move from one part of your answer to the next.

- however
- although
- on the other hand
- in comparison

Get your act together...

So there's <u>a lot to think about</u> in these what-if-you-were-the-director style questions. But they're a really good opportunity to give a good "<u>discussion</u>" — and the <u>more ideas</u> you have, the <u>better</u>.

DIRECTING QUESTIONS	# Appearance & Stage Effects

Directors have loads of <u>other stuff</u> to think about as well as how the actors should say their lines.

Mention What Sound and Lighting You'd Use

1) <u>Sound</u> can be used to create a <u>mood</u>. At the start of Act 4 Scene 1 you could have loads of <u>cheering</u> and <u>singing</u> to show the <u>excitement</u> and <u>optimism</u> about the wedding. When Claudio first accuses Hero it could go <u>dead quiet</u> — to show everyone's really <u>shocked</u>.

I said "lighting" not "lightning".

DIRECTOR

2) <u>Lighting</u> is also pretty crucial. At the start of Act 4 Scene 1, you could have <u>big, bright lights</u> to make it feel like a <u>sunny, happy day</u>. Then as the scene goes on the lights could <u>fade</u> so that it gets <u>duller and darker</u>, to show the increasing <u>tension</u>.

3) Remember to <u>explain</u> every suggestion you make. I know I sound like a broken record saying this, but you <u>absolutely, positively, definitely</u> have to do this. Honestly. I really, really mean it.

Say What Clothes They Should Wear

You can show you understand a scene by talking about the <u>costumes</u> you'd choose for it.

 e.g.
> In Act 4 Scene 1, I would have everybody dressed in the traditional way for a wedding. Hero would be wearing a white wedding dress to remind the audience that she is a virgin. It would also show that this is an important day for her and she wants to marry Claudio.

You <u>don't</u> have to stick to <u>old-fashioned</u> costumes. Lots of productions today use <u>modern clothes</u> and you can too — as long as you can show how they <u>suit the characters</u>.

Use Loads of Quotes (again)

Just like all the other types of question, you absolutely have to use <u>quotes</u> — but it's actually <u>dead easy</u> to stick a few quotes into these questions. <u>Follow these steps</u> and you're sorted:

I've got it wrong again, haven't I?

- say how you want the actors to speak and act, and what lighting and sounds you'd use

- find a quote that backs your idea up and write it down

- say why you'd do it (you won't get the marks otherwise)

Background music? Sound idea...

Just make sure you're still <u>answering the question</u> — if the question just says "What advice would you give to the actors?", don't go on about the lighting or makeup. But if it just says "How would you direct these scenes?", you can talk about pretty much <u>any aspect</u> of the production.

Revision Summary

So there you have it. Four types of exam question, and oodles of tips to help you with each one. Fair enough, some are easier than others — but you've got to be well prepared for any of those types of question, 'cos you just don't know what'll come up in the exam. And if the sight of the very word "exam" has you breaking out in a cold sweat, it's time to really get learning. Right, enough from me, let's have a butcher's at how much attention you've been paying in this section...

1) If you're writing about a character, is it a good idea or not to give a one-sided description of them?

2) What are the characters doing when they talk about each other?

   a) gossiping

   b) giving the audience messages

   c) showing off

3) What does "motivation" mean?

4) What does Shakespeare's "use of language" mean?

5) What's another word for mood?

6) What should you do if you get a theme question that seems really complicated?

   a) Read the question carefully and work out the main thing it's asking.

   b) Write a good answer on a different subject.

   c) Give up school and become a cattle rancher in Bolivia.

7) True or false? "You don't have to use quotes in theme questions."

8) Name four themes in Much Ado you might be asked about.

9) Explain what is meant by:

   a) anticipation

   b) dramatic irony

10) What does "body language" mean?

11) Give three words or phrases you could use to link different points together.

12) If you talk about clothes, should they always be old-fashioned costumes?

13) What do you absolutely, positively have to do every time you make a point in an essay?

   a) Explain the point and give evidence.

   b) Say what lighting you'd use.

   c) Play a fanfare.

The set scenes are the <u>only</u> scenes you need to know in real <u>detail</u>.
Make sure you know these two scenes <u>inside out</u>.

> Claudio has just announced he won't marry Hero because he thinks she's a slut. Claudio's stormed off, Hero's fainted, and everyone's in a frightful state. Friar Francis thinks Hero is innocent and comes up with a plan to cover up the scandal.

ACT 4 SCENE 1
A church

Present are LEONATO, FRIAR FRANCIS, BENEDICK, HERO, BEATRICE *and Attendants*

196-197 "Hold on a minute, and let me give you some advice."

FRIAR FRANCIS   Pause awhile,
And let my counsel sway you in this case.
Your daughter here the princes left for dead,

199-204 "Keep her at home in secret for a while and announce that she really is dead. Then pretend to mourn, hang an epitaph on the family tomb, and carry out a fake funeral."

Let her awhile be secretly kept in,
And publish it that she is dead indeed;   200
Maintain a mourning ostentation
And on your family's old monument
Hang mournful epitaphs and do all rites
That appertain unto a burial.

LEONATO   What shall become of this? What will this do?   205

206-209 "We'll change the nasty accusations for sorrow, which is better — but that's not my main reason for coming up with this strange plan. I'm hoping for an even better result."

FRIAR FRANCIS Marry, this well carried shall on her behalf
Change slander to remorse — that is some good —
But not for that dream I on this strange course,
But on this travail look for greater birth.

210-218 "We'll say that she died as soon as she was accused, which will make everyone pity her. We don't value what we have while we have it — it's only when we've lost something that we see the goodness that we ignored. That's how it will be with Claudio."

She dying, as it must be so maintained,   210
Upon the instant that she was accused,
Shall be lamented, pitied and excused
Of every hearer: for it so falls out
That what we have we prize not to the worth
Whiles we enjoy it, but being lacked and lost,   215
Why, then we rack the value, then we find
The virtue that possession would not show us
Whiles it was ours. So will it fare with Claudio.
When he shall hear she died upon his words,
The idea of her life shall sweetly creep   220
Into his study of imagination,

222-223 "and everything that was lovely about her in life will seem even more precious"

And every lovely organ of her life
Shall come apparelled in more precious habit,
More moving-delicate and full of life,
Into the eye and prospect of his soul,   225
Than when she lived indeed. Then shall he mourn,

226-227 "Then, if he has ever had true feelings of love, he will mourn"

If ever love had interest in his liver,
And wish he had not so accusèd her,
No, though he thought his accusation true.

230-232 "Trust me, things will work out better than expected."

Let this be so, and doubt not but success   230
Will fashion the event in better shape
Than I can lay it down in likelihood.

But if all aim but this be levelled false,
The supposition of the lady's death
Will quench the wonder of her infamy. 235
And if it sort not well, you may conceal her,
As best befits her wounded reputation,
In some reclusive and religious life,
Out of all eyes, tongues, minds and injuries.

233-238 "But even if the whole plan comes to nothing, at least her supposed death will distract people from the scandal. If the plan doesn't work, you can hide her in a convent."

BENEDICK   Signior Leonato, let the friar advise you, 240
And though you know my inwardness and love
Is very much unto the Prince and Claudio,
Yet, by mine honour, I will deal in this
As secretly and justly as your soul
Should with your body.

240-243 "Take the friar's advice, and though you know how close I am to Don Pedro and Claudio, I swear I will help carry out this plan."

LEONATO   Being that I flow in grief, 245
The smallest twine may lead me.

245-246 "I'm so upset, I'll do whatever I'm told."

FRIAR FRANCIS   'Tis well consented. Presently away;
For to strange sores strangely they strain the cure.
Come, lady, die to live. This wedding-day
Perhaps is but prolonged. Have patience and endure. 250

consented = agreed

248 "There are strange cures for strange illnesses."

Exeunt all but BENEDICK *and* BEATRICE

BENEDICK   Lady Beatrice, have you wept all this while?

BEATRICE   Yea, and I will weep a while longer.

BENEDICK   I will not desire that.

BEATRICE   You have no reason — I do it freely.

BENEDICK   Surely I do believe your fair cousin is wronged. 255

BEATRICE   Ah, how much might the man deserve of me
  that would right her!

Benedick and Beatrice are left alone — they admit they love each other. Beatrice asks Benedick to kill Claudio. He's not very keen to murder his friend, but agrees to challenge him to a duel.

256-257 "The man who saved her reputation would deserve so much from me!"

BENEDICK   Is there any way to show such friendship?

BEATRICE   A very even way, but no such friend.

even = straightforward

BENEDICK   May a man do it? 260

BEATRICE   It is a man's office, but not yours.

261 "It's a job for a man, but not for you."

BENEDICK   I do love nothing in the world so well as you: is
  not that strange?

BEATRICE   As strange as the thing I know not. It were as
  possible for me to say I loved nothing so well as you. 265
  But believe me not; and yet I lie not. I confess nothing,
  nor I deny nothing. I am sorry for my cousin.

BENEDICK   By my sword, Beatrice, thou lovest me.

BEATRICE   Do not swear and eat it.

269 "Don't swear to something and then take it back."

BENEDICK   I will swear by it that you love me, and I will   270
make him eat it that says I love not you.

BEATRICE   Will you not eat your word?

BENEDICK   With no sauce that can be devised to it.
I protest I love thee.

BEATRICE   Why, then, God forgive me!   275

BENEDICK   What offence, sweet Beatrice?

277-278 "You've stopped me just at the right moment. I was about to announce that I loved you."

BEATRICE   You have stayed me in a happy hour. I was
about to protest I loved you.

BENEDICK   And do it with all thy heart.

BEATRICE   I love you with so much of my heart that none   280
is left to protest.

BENEDICK   Come, bid me do anything for thee.

BEATRICE   Kill Claudio.

BENEDICK   Ha! Not for the wide world.

285 "You're killing me by refusing."

BEATRICE   You kill me to deny it. Farewell.   285

BENEDICK   Tarry, sweet Beatrice.

tarry = wait

BEATRICE   I am gone, though I am here. There is no
love in you. Nay, I pray you, let me go.

BENEDICK   Beatrice —

BEATRICE   In faith, I will go.   290

BENEDICK   We'll be friends first.

292-293 "You'd rather be my friend than fight my enemy."

BEATRICE   You dare easier be friends with me than fight
with mine enemy.

BENEDICK   Is Claudio thine enemy?

295-299 "Hasn't he been proved to be a total villain, who has lied about and dishonoured my relative, Hero? Oh, I wish I was a man! I mean, he led her on right until the last minute, and then told awful lies about her"

BEATRICE   Is he not approved in the height a villain, that   295
hath slandered, scorned, dishonoured my kinswoman?
O that I were a man! What, bear her in hand until they
come to take hands, and then, with public accusation,
uncovered slander, unmitigated rancour — O God, that I
were a man! I would eat his heart in the market-place.   300

BENEDICK   Hear me, Beatrice —

302 "What a ridiculous thing to say!"

BEATRICE   Talk with a man out at a window! A proper
saying!

BENEDICK   Nay, but Beatrice —

BEATRICE   Sweet Hero! She is wronged, she is
slandered, she is undone.   305

BENEDICK   Beat —

BEATRICE   Princes and counties! Surely, a princely
   testimony, a goodly count, Count Comfect, a sweet
   gallant, surely! O that I were a man for his sake! Or
   that I had any friend would be a man for my sake! But   310
   manhood is melted into curtsies, valour into
   compliment, and men are only turned into tongue, and
   trim ones too. He is now as valiant as Hercules that
   only tells a lie and swears it. I cannot be a man with
   wishing, therefore I will die a woman with grieving.   315

BENEDICK   Tarry, good Beatrice. By this hand, I love thee.

BEATRICE   Use it for my love some other way than
                                          swearing by it.

BENEDICK   Think you in your soul the Count Claudio hath
   wronged Hero?

BEATRICE   Yea, as sure as I have a thought or a soul.   320

BENEDICK   Enough, I am engaged. I will challenge him.
   I will kiss your hand, and so I leave you. By this hand,
   Claudio shall render me a dear account. As you hear of
   me, so think of me. Go, comfort your cousin. I must
   say she is dead, and so, farewell.   325

Exeunt

Count Comfect = *Count Sweeties*

310-315 "Manhood has been
watered down into politeness,
bravery into flattery, and men are
nothing but words. A man who
tells a lie and swears it's true is
now considered as brave as
Hercules. I can't make myself a
man by wishing for it, so I'll die of
grief as a woman."

engaged = *committed*

322-323 "I swear, Claudio will
pay dearly for what he has done."
Benedick shows his loyalties now
lie with Beatrice.

Everyone meets up for Claudio and Hero's wedding. Claudio doesn't know it's Hero until she takes her mask off. Benedick proposes to Beatrice and they decide to get married straight away. And then everyone dances off into the distance... ahhh...

ACT 5 SCENE 4
A room in Leonato's house

Enter LEONATO, ANTONIO, BENEDICK, BEATRICE, MARGARET, URSULA, FRIAR FRANCIS *and* HERO

FRIAR FRANCIS   Did I not tell you she was innocent?

2-6 "The Prince and Claudio, who accused her of the wrongdoing you heard us speak of, are innocent too. Margaret was a little bit to blame, although it seems that it was against her will."

LEONATO   So are the Prince and Claudio, who accused her
Upon the error that you heard debated.
But Margaret was in some fault for this,
Although against her will, as it appears   5
In the true course of all the question.

sort = are turning out

ANTONIO   Well, I am glad that all things sort so well.

8-9 "Me too, otherwise I would have been honour-bound to fight young Claudio over it."

BENEDICK   And so am I, being else by faith enforced
To call young Claudio to a reckoning for it.

10-12 "Right ladies, off you go into another room, and when I send for you, come back in wearing masks."

LEONATO   Well, daughter, and you gentlewomen all,   10
Withdraw into a chamber by yourselves,
And when I send for you, come hither masked.

13-16 "The Prince and Claudio are supposed to be here any minute. You know what to do, brother: pretend to be father to Hero and give her away to young Claudio."

The Prince and Claudio promised by this hour
To visit me. You know your office, brother:
You must be father to your brother's daughter   15
And give her to young Claudio.

Exeunt ladies

confirmed countenance = serious expression

ANTONIO   Which I will do with confirmed countenance.

18 "I need to ask you a favour."

BENEDICK   Friar, I must entreat your pains, I think.

FRIAR FRANCIS   To do what, signior?

20-22 "To make me, or break me — one of the two. Leonato, the truth is that your niece Beatrice rather likes the look of me."

BENEDICK   To bind me, or undo me — one of them.   20
Signior Leonato, truth it is, good signior,
Your niece regards me with an eye of favour.

23 "My daughter taught her to look like that. It's true."

LEONATO   That eye my daughter lent her. 'Tis most true.

24 "And I feel the same way about her."

BENEDICK   And I do with an eye of love requite her.

25-26 "I think you got that idea from me, Claudio and Don Pedro: but what is it you want to do?"

LEONATO   The sight whereof I think you had from me,   25
From Claudio and the Prince: but what's your will?

BENEDICK   Your answer, sir, is enigmatical,
But, for my will, my will is your good will
May stand with ours, this day to be conjoined
In the state of honourable marriage,   30
In which, good friar, I shall desire your help.

enigmatical = mysterious

LEONATO   My heart is with your liking.

28-30 "I want to marry Beatrice and I hope you'll wish us well."

FRIAR FRANCIS   And my help.
Here comes the Prince and Claudio.

Enter DON PEDRO *and* CLAUDIO *and two or three others*

DON PEDRO Good morrow to this fair assembly.

LEONATO Good morrow, Prince; good morrow, Claudio.   35
We here attend you. Are you yet determined
Today to marry with my brother's daughter?

> 36-37 *"We're waiting for you.
Are you still prepared to marry
my brother's daughter today?"*

CLAUDIO I'll hold my mind, were she an Ethiope.

> 38 *"I'll do as I've promised, even if
she's Ethiopian." Ethiopia was a semi-
mythical place for people alive in
Shakespeare's time — it's a bit like
saying 'even if she's a Martian'
nowadays.*

LEONATO Call her forth, brother — here's the friar ready.

Exit ANTONIO

DON PEDRO Good morrow, Benedick. Why, what's the
matter,   40
That you have such a February face,
So full of frost, of storm and cloudiness?

CLAUDIO I think he thinks upon the savage bull.
Tush, fear not, man, we'll tip thy horns with gold
And all Europa shall rejoice at thee,   45
As once Europa did at lusty Jove,
When he would play the noble beast in love.

> 43-47 *The 'savage bull' is Taurus,
the star sign for May. Jove is the
Roman name for the king of the
gods who, in Greek mythology,
turned himself into a bull to seduce a
girl called Europa. Claudio's saying
Benedick doesn't have to be worried
about getting married and having an
unfaithful wife — he can be a
successful lover like Jove. Claudio is
joking with Benedick.*

BENEDICK Bull Jove, sir, had an amiable low,
And some such strange bull leaped your father's cow,
And got a calf in that same noble feat   50
Much like to you, for you have just his bleat.

CLAUDIO For this I owe you. Here comes other reckonings.

Re-enter ANTONIO, *with the ladies masked*

Which is the lady I must seize upon?

> 48-51 *"When Jove was a bull, he
had a lovely bellow, and it seems
some bull mated with your father's
cow, and produced a calf a lot like
you, because you bellow in just the
same way."*

ANTONIO This same is she, and I do give you her.

CLAUDIO Why, then she's mine. Sweet, let me see your
face.   55

reckonings = *issues*

Who's the daddy?

LEONATO No, that you shall not, till you take her hand
Before this friar and swear to marry her.

CLAUDIO Give me your hand before this holy friar.
I am your husband, if you like of me.

HERO And when I lived, I was your other wife, *(unmasking)*   60
And when you loved, you were my other husband.

CLAUDIO Another Hero!

HERO   Nothing certainer.
One Hero died defiled, but I do live,
And surely as I live, I am a maid.

defiled = *disgraced*

maid = *virgin*

DON PEDRO The former Hero! Hero that is dead!   65

LEONATO She died, my lord, but whiles her slander lived.

> 66 *"She was only dead as long as
the lies about her were still believed."*

67-71 "I'll answer all your questions after the wedding, when I'll give you all the details of lovely Hero's death. In the meantime just take it all for granted and let's go into the chapel."

well-nigh = *just about*

83 "Only as a friend."

halting = *clumsy*

fashioned to = *created for*

92-93 "Come on, I'll marry you, but only because I feel sorry for you."

94-96 "I won't turn you down, but I swear I'm only giving in after some serious persuasion, and partly to save your life, because I was told you were wasting away."

FRIAR FRANCIS   All this amazement can I qualify,
    When after that the holy rites are ended,
    I'll tell you largely of fair Hero's death.
    Meantime let wonder seem familiar,   70
    And to the chapel let us presently.

BENEDICK   Soft and fair, friar. Which is Beatrice?

BEATRICE *(unmasking)*   I answer to that name. What is
                                    your will?

BENEDICK   Do not you love me?

BEATRICE   Why, no, no more than reason.

BENEDICK   Why, then your uncle and the Prince and Claudio   75
    Have been deceived — they swore you did.

BEATRICE   Do not you love me?

BENEDICK   Troth, no, no more than reason.

BEATRICE   Why, then my cousin, Margaret, and Ursula
    Are much deceived, for they did swear you did.

BENEDICK   They swore that you were almost sick for me.   80

BEATRICE   They swore that you were well-nigh dead for me.

BENEDICK   'Tis no such matter. Then you do not love me?

BEATRICE   No, truly, but in friendly recompense.

LEONATO   Come, cousin, I am sure you love the gentleman.

CLAUDIO   And I'll be sworn upon't that he loves her,   85
    For here's a paper written in his hand,
    A halting sonnet of his own pure brain,
    Fashioned to Beatrice.

HERO   And here's another
    Writ in my cousin's hand, stolen from her pocket,
    Containing her affection unto Benedick.   90

BENEDICK   A miracle! Here's our own hands against our
    hearts. Come, I will have thee, but, by this light, I take
    thee for pity.

BEATRICE   I would not deny you, but, by this good day, I
    yield upon great persuasion, and partly to save your life, 95
    for I was told you were in a consumption.

BENEDICK   Peace! I will stop your mouth. *(kisses her)*

DON PEDRO   How dost thou, Benedick, the married man?

BENEDICK   I'll tell thee what, Prince; a college of wit-crackers cannot flout me out of my humour. Dost thou think I care for a satire or an epigram? No. If a man will be beaten with brains, 'a shall wear nothing handsome about him. In brief, since I do purpose to marry, I will think nothing to any purpose that the world can say against it, and therefore never flout at me for what I have said against it, for man is a giddy thing, and this is my conclusion. For thy part, Claudio, I did think to have beaten thee, but in that thou art like to be my kinsman, live unbruised and love my cousin.

100

105

CLAUDIO   I had well hoped thou wouldst have denied Beatrice, that I might have cudgelled thee out of thy single life, to make thee a double-dealer, which, out of question, thou wilt be, if my cousin do not look exceeding narrowly to thee.

110

BENEDICK   Come, come, we are friends. Let's have a dance ere we are married, that we may lighten our own hearts and our wives' heels.

115

LEONATO   We'll have dancing afterward.

BENEDICK   First, of my word! Therefore play, music. Prince, thou art sad. Get thee a wife, get thee a wife! There is no staff more reverend than one tipped with horn.

120

Enter a Messenger

MESSENGER   My lord, your brother John is ta'en in flight, And brought with armed men back to Messina.

BENEDICK   Think not on him till tomorrow. I'll devise thee brave punishments for him. Strike up, pipers.

125

Dance.
Exeunt.

99-100 "A whole college of jokers couldn't taunt me out of my good mood."

satire = *witty poem*

epigram = *witty comment*

103-106 "Since I plan to marry, I won't listen to criticism. Don't tease me for what I've said about marriage in the past because men do change their minds, and that's all there is to it."

kinsman = *relative*

110-114 "I was hoping you'd turn Beatrice down so I'd have an excuse to beat you out of your single life, and force you to be a married man. You'll certainly be a married man unless Beatrice turns against you."

121 "There's no better walking stick than one with a horn handle" — in Shakespeare's day the horn was a well-known symbol for a man whose wife has had an affair.

122-123 "Your brother John has been captured as he tried to escape, and brought back to Messina under armed guard."

125 "I'll think you up some nasty ways of punishing him."

And they all lived happily ever after...

Yuk. I hate happy endings.

Section 7 — The Set Scenes

Index

Index

Complete Shakespeare plays
With brilliant notes, line by line

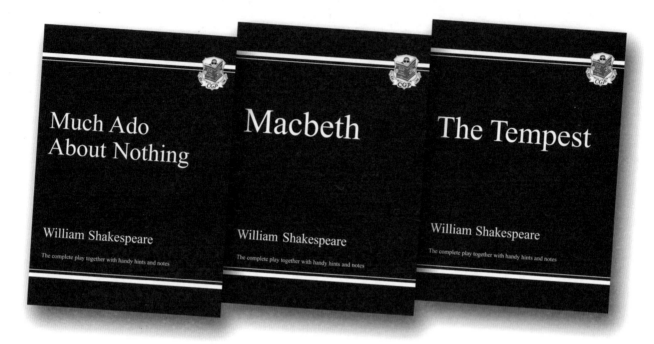

The full Shakespeare text

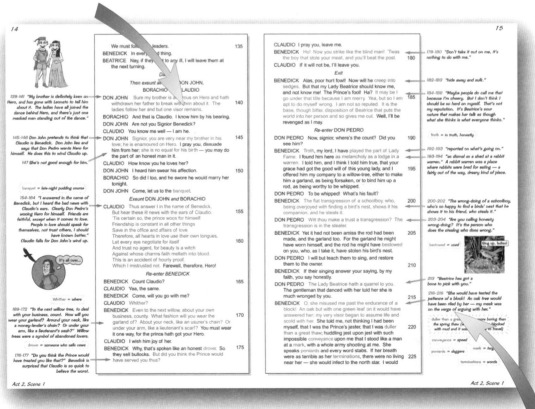

Clear, useful notes to
help explain the
language and imagery